MW01109043

My Father's Wisdom, My Mother's Love

A Spiritual Gift

by

Bill Vivio

authorHOUSE®

AuthorHouse™
1663 Liberty Drive, Suite 200
Bloomington, IN 47403
www.authorhouse.com
Phone: 1-800-839-8640

First published by AuthorHouse 6/26/2008

ISBN: 978-1-4343-7415-8 (sc)
ISBN: 978-1-4343-7416-5 (hc)

Library of Congress Control Number: 2008905393

Printed in the United States of America
Bloomington, Indiana

This book is printed on acid-free paper.

I once saw a plaque on a tree in the forest, which read:

"This tree gives glory to God by being a tree."[1]

I pray that this book, for which a tree gave us these pages and my words on these pages, will give glory to God as well...

Table of Contents

Acknowledgements   ix
Preface   xi
Introduction   xiii

1   *"Don't Fight It, Box It"*   1
2   *"How Much Do You Love Me?"*   5
3   *"It's Not What You Say; It's How You Say It"*   9
4   *"Don't Forget What It's Like to Be A Kid"*   15
5   *"Don't Grow Old, Grow Up"*   21
6   *"Don't Go Away Mad, Just Go Away"*   27
7   *"The More You Love, The More Divine*
        You Become"1   33
8   *"You Don't Have to Go to Cleveland to Have Fun"*   37
9   *"The Blind Leading The Blind"*   41
10 *"Grazie A Dio"*   45
11 *"The Eleventh Commandment...Don't*
        Get Caught"   49
12 *"He Ain't Feeling No Pain"*   55
13 *"Salute!"*   61
14 *"Alzarsi—A Wake-Up Call"*   67
15 *"Don't Worry, Be Happy"*   71
16 *"Abbondanza!"*   75
17 *"Old-Timer's Disease"*   79
18 *"He Is Right...Dead Right"*   85
19 *"First Things First"*   91
20 *"I Said to Myself, Said I"*   95
21 *"Teach The Right Way The First Time"*   99
22 *"Taking Care of Business"*   105
23 *"Two Wrongs Don't Make A Right"*   111
24 *"Faith, Hope, and Love"*   117
25 *"Que Sera Sera"*   123

End Notes   129
About the Author   135

Acknowledgements

When watching a sporting event on the television, people often see athletes interviewed who just won a race, scored a winning touchdown, or hit a home run to clinch a championship. In these interviews, they usually say statements like, "I want to thank God" or "I want to give glory to Jesus Christ who gave me this opportunity, or helped me accomplish this feat."

I feel I would be remiss if I did not offer thanks in much the same way. Therefore, I want to thank God the Father, His Son, Jesus Christ, and the Holy Spirit for Their help and inspiration in bringing forth this book.

This labor of love would never have come to completion without the loving support and input from my family. I would also like to thank and acknowledge my wife LuAnn, my daughters Nancy and Gina, and my son Victor, for their help.

I also want to thank the unnamed sources who have contributed to this book by inspiring me with their wisdom and ideas which have contributed to my education and experience. Unfortunately, in some cases, I may have forgotten who the original source was for my inspiration; however, throughout this book I do try to give credit where I can identify the source and give credit where credit is due.

Preface

The idea of this book came about as our family would gather and remember stories and anecdotes from my parents, Victor and Mary Vivio, better known to many in our family as "Gram" and "Pap." I wanted to write a book to honor their legacy. I wanted to share my memories of them with their children and grandchildren. I would also like my grandchildren and my nieces and nephews, and their children, to hear my parents' stories again and benefit by their wisdom with the hope that the memory of "my father's wisdom and my mother's love" will enrich their lives as much it has my own.

As I began to reflect more on my parents' lives, I saw parallels in their lives and the life and teachings of Jesus Christ. In particular, as I looked back on "my father's wisdom and my mother's love," I began to realize that they were both filled with the love of God the Father and the wisdom of the Holy Spirit. My parents were not particularly religious people, although they raised their children Roman Catholic and saw to it that we had the opportunity to attend Catholic schools. My brother Ed was even able to complete twelve years of Catholic education with their support. Beyond this religious foundation given us, the lessons they taught us, and the experiences they shared, were very much in line with the lessons taught by Jesus. So, I thought, why not write this book with a broader appeal for people everywhere who would benefit from *"My Father's Wisdom and My Mother's Love."*

Victor and Mary Vivio with their infant son Billy

1942

Introduction

As I write this book, I would like to share my thoughts and memories, and give credit to those who inspired ideas for this book and who are quoted within the text. I often quote from Henri Nouwen, Dr. Wayne Dyer, Paul the Apostle, and Jesus Christ, as well as scripture verses throughout the Bible. I apologize in advance for anyone quoted here that I forgot to mention or place in the end notes. I am more interested in conveying the thought, quote, or memory than giving credit to who may have first said or wrote it. I always liked what Ralph Waldo Emerson once wrote: "There is no limit to what can be accomplished if it doesn't matter who gets the credit."[1]

I once attended a sales seminar featuring the late great humorist and speaker Mr. Cavett Robert.[2] I love this statement that he made: "Over the years as I have given speeches, I would start out giving credit to certain persons that I was quoting. I started out quoting, 'As (insert name) once said, (then the quote).' After a few years, I would use the quote this way: 'as someone once said.' As more time passed by, I would just say, 'As I have always said...'" Cavett Robert was such a delightful speaker.

But I do try to give credit where I can, or when I remember who first said something. Besides, has anyone ever really had an original thought? Are not all of us a compilation of words, books, thoughts, and lessons learned in our lives? Well, I have been up to living this life for more than sixty years. I am sure as I learned along the way; I also forgot who I may have learned something from or who said what. So if I omitted a name or the proper source for something or not given credit where credit it is due, I apologize. If you wish to send me a note correcting the source of a quote, I would appreciate it. You my correct me, but please don't sue me.

I have wanted to write this book for more than ten years. My mom, Mary Vivio, passed away in 1982, and my dad, Victor Vivio, passed away in 1996. As I reflect on my life growing up, I am reminded over and over of "my father's wisdom and my mother's love." I have been blessed to have had them in my life, and fortunately, I am blessed with a good memory. Thank you for allowing me to share my memories with you here.

Bill Vivio

1
"Don't Fight It, Box It"

My dad had a wonderful outlook on life. I remember as a kid helping him in the family grocery store. There, he gave me many challenging responsibilities. I sometimes had difficulty putting the meat grinder "head" onto the grinder. Once, when this happened, I began to lose my temper, as I often did when I could not get an inanimate object to cooperate with me in its assemblage. As usual, I muttered under my breath, but I never cursed in front of my dad. However, he knew what I was thinking and he said, "Don't fight it, box it!"

This was a phrase that my dad learned as a young man while training to be a boxer. His trainer was a man named Jake Mintz. Jake would say this to his young fighters when they would lose their tempers in a fight and start to slug it out with their opponent (a street fighting style), leaving themselves open and vulnerable to their opponent. Jake would call out to them, "Don't fight 'em, box 'em!" My dad was not a very successful boxer, but he was very wise, and he used every lesson he learned to deal with life and likewise pass on these lessons to his children.

Sometimes it seems life isn't fair. Sometimes it seems we take two steps forward and one step back. It's easy to lose our perspective, get angry or try to force our agenda on life and others, only to find resistance from both. When that happens in life, "Don't fight it, box it." It may be better stated, "Finesse it." In dealing with life, like a good boxer, we would be wise to first see what life and others are giving us, then just "roll with the punches" and "look for an opening." In other words, in a difficult situation, don't fight it or curse it...finesse it. Better yet, look for the blessing in each situation. Look at what life might be offering, whether it is a lesson to be learned, an opportunity for growth, or an opening to another way to accomplish your goal.

I love a particular lesson I learned from Dr. Wayne Dyer, who taught this lesson in one of his earlier PBS presentations. I generally remember Dr. Dyer saying that we would be wise to reflect on the lines of the children's nursery song, "Row, Row, Row Your Boat."[1] (Sing along, if you like; you can even sing as a group "in a round.")

Row, row, row your boat,
Gently down the stream.
Merrily, merrily, merrily, merrily,
Life is but a dream.[2]

Dr. Dyer taught that in life we should follow the advice given in the song. Row your own boat, and don't try to control somebody else's boat. In life, controlling your own boat is enough. And how do we row our boat? We row it gently, down the stream, not trying to go upstream. We should go through life gently, joyfully, relishing each moment. Do not try to go against the tide or upstream; instead, go with the flow. Do not go up stream, but gently down the stream. And what should our attitude be? Joyful. Merrily, merrily, merrily. Why? Because life is but a dream.

I am not suggesting life is not serious business. But too many people take life and themselves way too seriously. So, like the nursery rhyme says, row your own boat and don't get too vexed over how others are rowing their boat through life. Don't fight it, it's the only life you have. Go gently down the stream of life, not upstream, not against the tide, but with the flow. Gently... And be gentle with yourself and others as you go. Be joyful and grateful for each passing day. Go merrily along your way, because for all we know, it may be just a dream.

I believe we are all a part of God's greatest dream that he chose to share with us. Unfortunately, so many of us go through life not dreaming, but sleepwalking and unaware of all of God's gifts, graces, and opportunities to love and be loved, while being filled with joy and harmony. Jesus tried to show us how to live and be aware of all life's abundance, opportunity, and blessings.

Jesus said, "...I came so that they might have life and have it more abundantly." John 10-10b (NAB)

Jesus is also often quoted in the scriptures as saying, "The kingdom of God is at hand" (e.g., Mat 1:15, Luke 21:31). I believe Jesus was trying to tell His followers that they have the ability and opportunity to experience God's kingdom of joy and love here and now if we choose. If we choose to live as Jesus did, we will live lives centered in the grace of God the Father, living and loving one another as God's children, and always ready to heal and forgive all those that we encounter.

To paraphrase William J. O'Malley, S.J., from his book *The Pursuit of Happiness: Evolving a Soul,*[3] "Live life abundantly in what time you have...Don't bother too much whether there is life after death. Be too busy making sure that there is life before death."

"The kingdom of God is at hand."

Mark 1:15 (NAB)

Choose to wake up and start living life...and "don't fight it, box it."

Thanks, Dad.

2
"How Much Do You Love Me?"

Someone once said, "Truth without love is brutality, Love without truth is hypocrisy."[1]

The first memory of my mom is of a pretty, smiling, loving woman with eyes that revealed pride in her children and an approving smile when she spoke. Now, this is not to say that she never was disappointed in some of my actions. When she was upset, she would purse her lips in obvious disapproval of my actions. From my earliest memories, I recall my mom playing hand games with us, such as "patty cake" and the like. Those games would end with my mom asking, "How much do you love me?" My answer would be "Thisss much!" And I would stretch out my little arms as wide as I could possibly stretch them. Then I would ask her, "How much do you love me?" And she would answer, "Thisss much!" And she would stretch out her arms as far as she could. We would go back and forth with this same question and answer, each of us trying to outstretch the other, until we finally broke out into laughter.

A number of years ago, after my ordination as a deacon, I was assigned to Saint Helen's Parish in Glendale, Arizona. I was helping with preparing our young teenagers for the Church sacrament of Confirmation. While they were on their Confirmation retreat, someone gave them a handout titled *A Love Letter From Jesus*. I remember it being quite a beautiful letter that concluded with Jesus asking the question, "How much do I love you?" And when you turned the page over there was a picture of Jesus spreading out his arms as if he was hanging on a cross, and the caption read, "This much!"

Well, I don't have to tell you what fond memories that image brought back to me. Ever since reading that handout, each time I look at a crucifix with the arms of Jesus spread out, I am reminded of how much he loves me. I am especially moved each time I look at a large, sometimes life size crucifix in a church.

As a lifelong budding artist, I always loved to draw, trace, and color whatever was of latest interest to me. I remember one event when I was about five years old, when it must have been the Easter season. I know this because the Easter Bunny occupied a lot of my thinking, and I had decided to draw a family of Easter bunnies. The only problem with this idea was that I drew the bunnies with a black crayon on our yellow wallpaper in the living room. Although the drawing was pretty good, my mom became quite angry. She was the angriest that I have ever seen her. She scolded me, and I remember being upset with my mom and myself for drawing on the wallpaper. I cried and pouted for a while, and I did not speak to my mom the rest of the evening. At bedtime I remember my dad carried me up the stairs to my bedroom. As I was looking over his shoulder I saw my mom standing at the bottom of the stairs looking up at me. She called up to me, "Good night Billy!" to which I did not respond.

Next, she used that disarming question which she would always use after she said good night. Knowing that I was still upset about the earlier wallpaper incident, she asked, "How much do you love me?" I remember shaking my head, gesturing "No." As I did, I squeezed my arms as tightly as I could against my chest. As long as I live, I will never forget the look of disappointment and heartbreak on my mother's face as I did that...I'm sorry, Mom.

That story makes me think of how often we see the image of Jesus on the cross saying, "This is how much I love you. How much do you love me?" How often do we shrug, or shake our head no, and embrace only ourselves, like an angry five-year-old child?

"...living the truth with love..."

Eph. 4:15a (NAB)

3
"It's Not What You Say; It's How You Say It"

My dad used this saying to teach a lesson about life to his children. It was a simple but very important lesson that I wish more people would learn. My dad would say, "You can say anything, if you have a smile on your face." He would say, "You can call me an S.O.B., but you better have a smile on your face when you say it." What he meant was that you can voice your opinion and make your feelings known by being assertive, and can say just about anything if you do so with *love and respect*.

Another thought about this lesson is that what you say and how you say it can resonate with others. I once had a mentor, Fr. J.J. McCarthy (O Carm)[1], who said, "If you have two guitars and place one on each side of a room, opposite one another, and then strike a note on one of the guitars, the string of the other guitar will begin to slightly resonate (vibrate) with the first." He used this example to encourage his students of spiritual direction to share our spiritual experiences and stories with others. The reason being, our spiritual experiences will resonate with another's spiritual experience and theirs will resonate with ours. This will increase and enrich the spiritual experience for both parties. By sharing your experience, you take ownership of that experience and you will reinforce and remind others of theirs.

So here is a spiritual experience that I would like to share with you. It happened over fifty years ago when I was around fifteen years old. I was attending high school in Pittsburgh, and each day after school, I would take a streetcar from downtown to the north side of the city where my parents had a grocery store. I would help them throughout the remainder of the day by stocking shelves and doing other chores until it was time to close the store and go home. One day on the streetcar ride to the store, there was heavy traffic, and the streetcar moved slowly through the traffic in a stop-and-go fashion. As we crossed over one of many bridges to the north side, across the Allegheny River, moving at a stop-and-go pace, I was staring out the window, kind of daydreaming. I guess I was thinking about my life, my future, and my understanding of God, when suddenly I felt the powerful presence of the Holy Spirit. I felt as if I were glowing, although I am sure that I was not. I had a powerful sense of being loved *unconditionally*. I felt as if I was just basking in God's love. This experience has stayed with me all of my life, and to this day it affects my relationships with God and others. It helped me to fully appreciate now what Jesus said:

As the Father has loved me, so have I loved
you. Now remain in my love. If you obey my
commands, you will remain in my love, just as I
have obeyed my Father's commands and remain
in his love.

John 15:9-10 (NAB)

After that experience, I naturally got caught up with the things of life like everyone else, but now always knowing and sensing that I am loved...

About thirty years after that experience is when I was involved with a group of Catholic spiritual directors, and one of our mentors was the earlier-mentioned Fr. McCarthy. He offered many lessons in spiritual direction. He encouraged us to reflect back on our lives and think about a time when we may have encountered God. Fr. McCarthy encouraged us to think about these reflections and share our stories with others, so that they no longer swirled around in our heads or memories but were brought out into the world of others. If they stay inside us, we might begin to think that they did not really happen or that they were part of our imagination...or they're my own creation...that maybe we were just dreaming. But once we bring our experiences into the light and share them, we make them real and nobody can take them away from us. Besides, I think God wants us to share our stories as a way of sharing our faith and bolstering each other's faith.

Once, I was telling a prayer group my story and encouraging others to tell their stories, when one woman named Claudette shared a story of an angel who drove a Mercedes Benz. My friend said that once a week she would go into downtown San Diego, California, to work at St. Vincent De Paul's kitchen to prepare and serve meals for the homeless. One of the homeless women, whose name was Lucy, used to come in and help with the preparation and serve food too. Now, despite Lucy's situation, she was a very cheerful person, always helping and encouraging others there. Everyone who knew Lucy appreciated and admired how she would assist others who were in the same situation as herself. One day, Claudette was in the kitchen preparing dinner when Lucy came in, not smiling and or as joyful as usual, but instead very sad and fearful. When asked what was wrong, Lucy said, "I lost everything. I have nothing!" She went on to explain that when she came to the dining room that morning, she parked her grocery cart, filled with all of her clothes, her coat, and other personal items, in the side yard. This yard was supposed to be secured, so that the homeless visitors could leave their possessions there while in the dining hall. After lunch and cleaning up, Lucy went out to retrieve her cart only to discover that all her worldly possessions had been stolen. Devastated, she searched downtown San Diego in vain for her cart. Later she returned to the dining hall to help serve the evening meal. She shared her story with the kitchen help and said she didn't know what she was going to do that night, since it was so cold outside. The next day, Lucy came in all smiles and filled with joy. The old Lucy was back. The ladies in the kitchen wanted to know what happened during the previous night. She went on to tell this story.

After dinner the night before, she and another homeless woman went searching for her things. As the evening grew late, she and her friend decided to stop and find a place to spend the night. Her friend had an extra coat for Lucy to wear and some cardboard in her cart for Lucy to lie upon. So they picked out what looked like a safe place, when suddenly, Lucy saw a shiny Mercedes Benz pull up to the curb. The window went down on the passenger side and a woman's voice called out to them from inside the car. The woman told them to come closer because she had something for them. As they approached the car, the woman inside pushed two new, heavy-duty, high-quality bedrolls through the window to Lucy and her friend. The woman's voice inside the car said, "It's going to get very cold tonight. I thought you could use these." The window went back up and the car drove away. Lucy said, "We were visited by an angel last night, an angel in a Mercedes Benz."

When we share our stories, we take ownership of them and give them to others to experience as well. I will never forget Lucy and her angel.

There is a story about a young Catholic priest, newly ordained, just out of seminary and beginning his first assignment at a very busy parish. His parish should have had three or four priests to minister, but due to the shortages in the priesthood; there were only the young priest and the older pastor, a man of seventy years of age, in attendance there. Although the young priest was very energetic and worked very hard to keep up with the parish needs, he was becoming exasperated with his duties. So he went to the older priest for advice. The young priest said, "It's hard to complete my daily chores and minister to the people. As you know, Father, I smoke cigarettes, but I don't have time to smoke, and I don't have time to pray. I was wondering, Father, do you think it would be suitable if I smoke while I pray?" The older pastor said, "Why goodness, no. Prayer is time to be spent with God, and you should not smoke while you pray." So the younger priest went away sad to ponder what the older priest had shared. The next day when the two priests were having lunch together, the young priest asked the older priest, "Father, do you think it would be suitable if I prayed while I was taking a smoking break?" The older priest said, "Why yes. That would be an excellent time to pray; better than what would otherwise be a waste of time on a bad habit."

"He who frames the question wins the debate" (Randall Terry).[2]

And again, "It's not what you say; it's how you say it." Vic Vivio

And so we learn in this lesson to be sure of two things. First, respect the Spirit of God who dwells in God's people and share Him with others. And second, when we speak, we should always speak with love and respect for others.

4

"Don't Forget What It's Like to Be A Kid"

My dad often would say, "Don't forget what it's like to be a kid," when someone would complain about their own children or about children in general. Often as we change and grow, and mature into adulthood, we tend to forget what we were like when we were children.

When I was a child, I used to talk as a child,
think as a child, reason as a child; when I
became a man, I put aside childish things.

I Corinthians 13:11 (NAB)

But in putting away childish things, don't forget what it's like to be a child. Remember those days fondly. Don't forget the joy and playfulness of childhood, nor the hopes, dreams, and a life without care. Remembering will help you to think upon your roots and ideals before you get caught up in living according to other people's rules and ideals. "Don't forget what it's like to be a kid" is the lesson I try to think of when I'm around children, and at times when they frustrate me. I often work with children in the preparation for receiving their Sacraments of Initiation for the Catholic Church, those being the Sacraments of Baptism, Confirmation, and First Eucharist (or first Communion). In working with these children, I can

15

see they want the sacraments, but *not* the sacrament's preparation class. They would rather be somewhere else playing with friends, participating in sports, playing video games, or just watching TV...almost anything but attending class. They may want to laugh, talk, and be generally disruptive to the class. I may begin to become upset and take control of the class as I must, but then, I remember what I was like as a kid. I remember going to Catholic school and preparing for my first Communion while attending the second grade at St. Andrews Catholic School. Sometimes when you remember what it was like to be a kid, you will also remember some important life lessons that you learned along the way.

I remember the morning of my first Communion. It was in the month of May, on the feast of Jesus' ascension into heaven. I remember that First Communion at St. Andrews was always on the Feast of the Ascension, and it was always a school holiday. Mass was to begin at 9:00 a.m., so our teacher, (we'll just call her Sister Geraldine), had all of the children gather in her classroom at 8:00 a.m. We were all very excited. The little girls were wearing their new white dresses and all of the boys were wearing their new white suits: white shirt, white tie, white shoes, and white socks. This was back in 1949, when people made sure to dress their children appropriately for very special occasions. And we felt very special, very happy, and excited. As we waited, I remember all of a sudden we heard Sister Geraldine scream in shock at a little girl in our class. The young girl was chewing gum, and Sister came down on her like a ton of bricks. Now, this was not just a case where a child got caught chewing gum in class. No, this was much more severe. In those days, anyone wishing to receive Communion had to fast by having no food or drink from midnight until the Eucharist was received. You may be aware that this is where the term "breakfast" comes from. You did not have breakfast until after you had gone to mass and received Communion, and then returned home to "break the fast."

On a side note, Easter is a major feast day in the church. We used to wear our very best clothes, even better then our Sunday best. Many people purchased new outfits and even Easter bonnets to go to church for this very special holy day. After the big celebration of the risen Lord at mass, we would go out to someplace special, dressed in all of our finery. We would enjoy a meal that was more than just breakfast. It was a combination of breakfast and lunch known as Easter brunch today. It is still a big day and celebration for many families. I am surprised at how many people celebrate Easter the same way today, except that now many people today just pass on morning mass and the celebration of the risen Lord to go straight to the "Easter brunch." I'm not making any judgment here, just an observation.

So, let's go back to 1949, before the church changed the rule of fasting from midnight on to prepare yourself to receive the Lord in Communion. There, in the second grade at St. Andrews, when Sister Geraldine was furious at the little girl, Sister made the girl spit out the gum into the trash, but she also ordered her to remain in her seat at her desk until after mass. The little girl would not be receiving her first Communion with her classmates. As the other students witnessed the encounter, you could have heard a pin drop in the classroom. All of the children were dumb-stricken that this girl would not be going to mass with the rest of us. We lined up to go in procession from our classroom over to the church, all of us quiet and concerned for our classmate. I remember entering the church from the rear; as the music started, all of the people stood up. All of the parents and families of these children were so happy and proud of them. I'm sure we felt their joy and pride. But then, I thought of the parents of the little girl we left back at the classroom. What must they be thinking? Their daughter was not with her class, and she would not be receiving her first Communion that day. I don't know what happened to the little girl or her parents. In those days, however, the Church ruled, and what Sister said was final. Maybe the parents had it out with Sister Geraldine or the priest afterward? Maybe they pulled their child out of school? As I think back on this incident, it helps me to remember what it was like to be a kid. Today, Catholics only have to fast for one hour prior to receiving Communion. I don't know what the ruling would be on chewing gum. After all, when you are chewing gum, you're not consuming food. I wish Sister Geraldine had given that little girl some slack that day. In any case, we all learned a lesson that day we would not soon forget.

I have forgotten the name of the little girl, but I will never forget the incident. Whoever you are, if you are reading this, and this kind of injury happened to you, I want you to know that I have not forgotten you and how I felt compassion for you and your family back on that day. I would understand if you left the Church and never received Communion again in your life. But I would say to you that if I could feel compassion for you at age seven, how much more our Heavenly Father feels compassion for you always. Please do not keep away from Him or His gift to you in the Eucharist. We all need that connection with the Divine.

To Sister Geraldine's credit, she told our class that after we received our first Communion, we would be filled with Jesus Christ. She said that in our state of Holy Innocence we should go home after mass and hug our mother and father, because for them, it would be like embracing Christ himself. But, I was such a grouch that day after my first Communion mass that I forgot to hug my parents and give them the opportunity to embrace Christ like Sister Geraldine had suggested. Days later, I did remember what she told me, and sheepishly told my dad that I forgot to hug him. Because my dad never forgot what it was like to be a kid, he smiled and embraced me, despite his disappointment.

As for the rest of us, I believe we should never forget what it is like to be a kid. Don't forget what it is like to live life a little lighter, a little more joyfully. Laugh a little more, play a little more, and always remember that, as a believer, you are a child of God.

It has been said, "Christians forget Christ's joy and the Buddhists forget the Buddha's sorrow,"[1] but don't you ever forget what it is like to be a kid.

5
"Don't Grow Old, Grow Up"

"Others may give you authority, but only you can take responsibility."[1]

S.I. Hayakawa

That day, after my first Communion Mass, I remember that I rushed home to change out of my white Communion suit and put on the brand-new baseball uniform that my grandmother had given me as a my first Communion gift. When we all arrived home, my mom had other plans. She said the first thing I had to do was to pose for family pictures (*ugh*), and visit with the family for a while. Meanwhile, my boyhood friend, Virgie Petrocelli, was waiting for me on my front steps wearing *his* new baseball uniform. I don't know how long I had to put up with the agony of complying with my mom's agenda, but from my long face and slouching posture in those pictures, you could see that I was not going along with her happily. This was one of those times that my mom would complain to my dad about my negative attitude. As she was getting quite upset with me, my dad would just say, "Now Mary, don't forget what it was like to be a kid."

My parents were very busy with their grocery store, and they gave my brother, sister, and I certain jobs and chores to do and expected to take on much of what would be considered grown-up responsibilities today. In our house you had to grow up before you grew old.

My dad could only teach us what he had learned in life. As I think back now, I realize that he taught us our first lessons about business and salesmanship. As it turns out, all three of us later made a very good living in the sales profession.

Back in the 1930s a new soda pop was introduced to the city of Pittsburgh. It was Pepsi-Cola. Dad was so proud of the part that he played in Pepsi's success. My dad drove a Pepsi-Cola truck around the city introducing Pepsi to the public. And although he did drive a truck and was a proud member of the Teamsters Union, Local 249, he was really much more than a truck driver. He said these men were called Driver-Salesman. And that is what they were. These drivers even took sales training classes. One lesson my dad learned was; "Sell the sizzle and not the steak!" He would explain that we kids should do the same with anything we might be selling. Today sales trainers teach to sell using features and benefits. My dad told us that in those days, Coca-Cola was the best-selling soft drink in America, so Pepsi decided to go after the younger generation of customers. Because Pepsi came in a 12-ounce bottle instead of Coke's old-fashioned 6-ounce bottle, the larger bottle had more appeal to young people. Pepsi exploited this difference in a popular radio jingle that went like this:

Pepsi Cola hits the spot, twice as much and that's a lot,

Twice as much for a nickel, too, Pepsi Cola is the drink for you.

If you remember that jingle, you may have been one of the younger generations Pepsi was appealing to...but now, you are old. However, like me, you had the privilege of being one of the new *Pepsi Generation.*

Let's go back to the grocery store and the lessons in salesmanship it gave us. Back then, we learned discipline and respect as we worked for our parents. Sometimes, especially around the holidays, we learned to work very hard without complaining. We learned that the customer was always right, and to act in a certain way around customers. After I retired recently, I realized how the discipline and salesmanship I had learned from my parents contributed so much to my success in life as I grew older and moved on.

On the matter of growing up and moving on to adulthood, we must also grow up and move on in matters of faith and our relationship with our Heavenly Father. I have noticed that many people stay stuck in the mindset of a young child in matters of faith. I am not criticizing those with childlike faith, because as Jesus said, "...the kingdom of God belongs to such as these" Luke 18:16*b* (NAB). No, I am speaking of those with childish faith. Those whose piety is still coming from what they understood in their childhood. For example, when teachers like Sister Geraldine ruled the roost, no one would dare to question something an authority figure said. Back then, if you asked, "Why is that so?" The answer was always, "Because Sister said so." End of debate. But those who do not question stay stuck in the faith of a child. These are folks who have not taken a Christian education class or a Bible study since grade school. They have a grade-school understanding of their faith and church. In a sense, these men and woman have not grown out of their first communion dresses and white suits, spiritually speaking. What we all need is a mature relationship with Jesus Christ.

I think that my main responsibility as a spiritual director is to invite you to look at your relationship with God. Is it a relationship between God and the man or woman He created you to be? Or are you like a small child who cannot appreciate the unconditional love that God has for all of us? Do you value Jesus, who sacrificed so much for us? Do you appreciate the Holy Spirit, our Advocate who has so many gifts for us? His gifts help us live our lives as devoted disciples, fulfilling our call and vocation in life; living our lives abundantly.

By growing into a more mature spiritual relationship with God (Father, Son, and Holy Spirit) we will experience all that we are called to be, and all that life has to offer us. So go ahead take responsibility for the faith given to you by God, and hopefully handed down to you by your parents.

In addition to inviting you to experience a more mature relationship with your Heavenly Father, I also want you to remember what it was like to be a kid (see previous chapter), so that you can experience *child-like*, not *child-ish* faith. Remember what it was like to be a kid who first experienced things of a spiritual nature. Remember when you first experienced the infant Jesus at Christmastime and all of the awe and wonder that you felt about Him then. Now you possibly desire a mature relationship with God and still want to have the awe and wonder in your soul toward our Heavenly Father, who reveals something new and awesome regularly to those who are looking for it. The problem with childish faith is that it may never mature into a fully actualized spiritual faith.

To extend this idea, let's examine how when some children discover that Santa Claus or the Easter Bunny are not real, they grow cynical and begin to think that the same is true of Jesus Christ and His life-and-death story. These people cannot trust the good news of Jesus Christ. If there is an argument against teaching your kids about Santa Claus, this would be it. But I know Santa's story is based in part on history and mostly on fiction to help capture the imagination of children. I know that it is done out of tradition so that somehow children can be able to celebrate the joy of Christmas handed down to us through the centuries. But I have often wondered how many kids after finding out the truth about Santa Claus might say, "You fooled me once. You are not going to fool me twice with the story of Jesus Christ." "The story of Santa Claus sounded too good to be true, and then there is the story of Jesus Christ that you want me to believe too." You know what they say, "If it sounds too good to be true, it probably is."

I fear this misunderstanding would be especially true in homes that lack love. If there is no love in a home, how can one believe in a loving Heavenly Father? If they never experience a loving father, how can they believe one exists? The kids here might go along with their parents' belief and they will go to church with their parents, but before long they might say; "Hey, you fooled me once, you're not going to fool me twice." And by the time they reach maturity, they let their childish ideas of God and religion fall away, and join the cynical world where there are many others who have lost their faith, or *never* had faith to begin with.

Thomas Merton wrote, "Humility is absolutely necessary if one is to avoid acting like a baby all of one's life."[2] Or in other words, you might grow old before you grow up.

6
"Don't Go Away Mad, Just Go Away"

"As a result of this, many of his disciples returned to their former way of life, and no longer accompanied him. Jesus then said to the Twelve, "Do you also want to leave?"

John 6: 66-67 (NAB)

Sometimes when we are growing up, we are disappointed and we get upset about many things. I would often get upset when my dad said no to me, or he when would not allow a certain behavior, or permit me to do something, or go somewhere I wanted to go. I would be disappointed and begin to get upset. My dad would say, "Hey, Bill, don't go away mad, just go away!" That phrase of his was always disarming to me and my reaction was always to smile when he said it. He had a way of doing that to me. He always had a quick witty phrase or a saying that would fit the occasion. If I was acting inappropriately in a particular setting or location my dad would say, "Where do you think you are, at home or some other dirty place?" These silly, but thought-provoking phrases, always made me laugh in spite of myself. My dad used phrases like these so that I would not take life or myself too seriously. If I pressed an issue too far, he

27

would gently remind me that I was approaching the end of my rope and the end of his patience. He might say, "Which side do you want to fall on?" meaning, *after I hit you.* Once more, my dad was using humor to let me know he was the boss. He had a way of saying these things without being offensive. I, on the other hand, do not have this gift. Once I was driving my best friend home after we had been out for the evening. We purchased some fast food at a drive-thru on the way, and we ate as we drove home. My buddy finished with one of the food wrappers and tossed it on the floor of my car and I said, "Hey, where do think you are, home or some other dirty place?" Well, my friend did not take that very well, and he immediately told me that was an insult to him, his family, and his mother in particular. We did not talk to one another for the rest of the ride home, even though I apologized and tried to tell him it was just an attempt at humor. He was very upset, and to this day I don't know why. His mother kept a very neat and clean home. Maybe he did not think so, and I rubbed him the wrong way on a sore spot. Or maybe I should have said when he got out of the car, "Don't go away mad, just go away." Well, anyway, let's just chalk that lesson up to "It's not what you say, it's how you say it." I just do not have my dad's gift for wry humor.

My dad would use other phrases to impart wisdom or humor such as, "Always put the empties away." This was my dad's way of saying you should always clean up after yourself, especially if you and your friends are drinking beer from bottles. He did not want my mom or anyone else to be able to count how many beers he drank. For him, it was a privacy issue. The same is true of some of his Italian sayings. I hope I get this right. *"Non-da-cuta-tuoi"* in my dad's dialect, or *"affare non sono i tuoi,"* in Italian, meaning, mind your own business. "Not too much *Confidenza"* or *"non troppo molto Confidenza"* in Italian, means "don't take him into your confidence", or "watch what you say to him." In English it may mean something like, "Don't get too chummy with strangers." My dad shared these words of wisdom long before the movies *The Godfather* and *The Godfather Part II* came out with the following pearls of wisdom:

"Never let anyone outside the family know what you're thinking." Don Vito Corleone[1,]

and

"Keep your friends close, but your enemies closer." Michael Corleone[2]

Even Jesus said, "...do not let your left hand know what your right is doing." Matthew 6:3 (NAB)

Whether it's my mom, dad, the Bible stories, books, or movies, I look for words of wisdom wherever I can find them. I have always tried as much as possible to observe and learn from others around me. I especially try to learn from their mistakes. I figure that if I can learn from others' mistakes, I am that much farther ahead of avoiding the pain and suffering they had to pay for those mistakes. Others' mistakes are some of the reasons why I have never experimented with drugs or committed adultery against my wife. I've learned from others that it's just not worth it. It's the same in matters of faith. You either have the gift of faith or you don't. But I notice that some who have the gift of faith try to make sense of it all, and they forget that it is called "faith," not "knowledge." For instance, many people have a problem relating to God as our Heavenly Father because he does not measure up to our image of what God should be. They want to make God into our image while forgetting that we were made in His (Genesis 1:26). Think about that for a moment:

His Image...
His Imagination...
His Creative Thought...
His Creation.

Henri Nouwen once wrote, "Incarnation and Eucharist are two great examples of God's tremendous love for us."[3]

How else could He capture our imagination....and enrich our faith? Jesus did capture the imagination of those closest to him.

"But there are some of you who do not believe." Jesus knew from the beginning the ones who would not believe and the one who would betray him. And he said, "For this reason I have told you that no one can come to me unless it is granted him by my Father." As a result of this, many (of) his disciples returned to their former way of life and no longer accompanied him. Jesus then said to the Twelve, "Do you also want to leave?" Simon Peter answered him, "Master, to whom shall we go? You have the words of eternal life. We have come to believe and are convinced that you are the Holy One of God." John 6:64-69 (NAB)

Their belief was such that they were willing to give their lives for it. Ironically...Jesus wouldn't say this...but my dad would have said to the departing disciples, "Don't go away mad, just go away."

7

"The More You Love, The More Divine You Become"[1]

In memory of Fr. Dominic Valentino (1919–2001)

Someone once said that conditional love is an oxymoron. I believe this statement is so true, for love that is conditional is not love, but something else. It may pass for love; it may substitute for love, but it is not love.

I guess I learned to love from my mom, whose love was never conditional, although she was not one to talk about "love" very much. She lived it by the love in her heart and the joy in her life. You could look at her smile, look into her eyes, and see how much she loved you.

My mom, and her mother, always had love and joy to give you when you saw them. Sometimes I don't know why they were so joyful and loving, because many people who had lived their lives would have become bitter and unloving victims of society.

My grandmother, Helen, gave birth to five children; one boy died at an early age. She was left to raise four children on her own once her husband abandoned the family for other pursuits during the Great Depression. Grandma did the best she could to hold things together as a single mother in those very difficult times. She took in ironing and did housecleaning for those who were working on jobs outside the home and could afford it. My mom, the second oldest child, and her older sister, my Aunt Toots, helped their mother as best they could to care for their home and the other children.

The Depression Era was hard on everyone. I remember my mom telling me this very sad story. One day, as she was coming home from school with her girlfriends, she was shocked and embarrassed to see that the sheriff had come and evicted her family from their apartment. Grandma did not have money for the rent, and all of her family's furniture and belongings were out on the sidewalk. I guess if you begin your adolescent years at the bottom like that; there is no place to go except up. My mom lived each day with an attitude of gratitude. Someone once said, "If you want to go to heaven you must be happy on earth."[2]

My mom showed me how to live, love, and be happy in life. These were the parting words that Jesus said to his disciples: "Love one another as I love you." John 15:12*b* (NAB)

When I give instruction to parents who bring their children for baptism, I remind them of those words of Jesus. I tell the parents that other than our Heavenly Father, no one loves these children more than they do. Just think of the potential of your children if they are raised in an atmosphere of unconditional love. Your children will grow in love to be adults who are men and woman of total love. And they will be a blessing to all who meet them and know them. They will be unselfish in sharing their love with others, because they will be full of love and sure of their love. They will not hold back or hoard their love, because they are love. The ability to love like this is in all Christians…it is just that, unfortunately, many people are not aware of it.

You should know, as a Christian that you are a blessing and you take that blessing everywhere you go, to each place that you enter. Each Christian is a blessing for one another… I was inspired to write the following for my wife on the fortieth anniversary of our wedding day.

"Love…you can use it, give it away, or not if you choose…
but love, you can never lose."

As a believer in Jesus Christ, you cannot lose love because you are love. You were created in love; you were created in the image of God, who is love. You are love, and you are a blessing. You can bless each experience in your life if you choose to do so.… Do so!

8

"You Don't Have to Go to Cleveland to Have Fun"

My dad first used these words when his buddies would want to take a bus full of friends and a keg of beer and travel from Pittsburgh, Pennsylvania, to Cleveland, Ohio, to watch the Steelers play the Browns. He would say, "You don't have to go to Cleveland to have fun."

Thereafter, it became a favorite saying of his anytime someone would have an idea to travel to some location to experience something different. My dad was a "bloom where you are planted" sort of guy. He also believed that "You don't have to go to church to pray." He did not attend church regularly, but he had a deep and close relationship with God, and he spoke of God often. He showed his faith especially by the way he lived his life. I share this not to discourage you from attending church services regularly, but instead, to encourage you to pray always and everywhere. Let your prayer to God "bloom where you are planted." Because God is everywhere.

> *He was praying in a certain place, and when he had finished, one of his disciples said to him, "Lord, teach us to pray just as John taught his disciples."*
>
> *Luke 11:1 (NAB)*

I love the example that Jesus gave us. He did not just say when or how we should pray, but by His example, He showed us how prayer and praise of His Heavenly Father were never far from His lips. He taught us to not only speak to Him informally, as a child might speak to their dad, but He also showed us to always give thanks.

> *"Jesus went to the synagogue regularly, as was his custom on the Sabbath day."*
>
> *Luke 4:16 (NAB)*

My dad did not think you had to go to church to pray, because he said many of the people there were fakers. Jesus might have used the word "hypocrites," as the Gospel of Matthew states:

> *"When you pray, do not be like the hypocrites, who love to stand and pray in the synagogues and on street corners so that others may see them. Amen, I say to you, they have received their reward. But when you pray, go to your inner room, close the door, and pray to your Father in secret. And your Father who sees in secret will repay you. In praying, do not babble like the pagans, who think that they will be heard because of their many words. Do not be like them. Your Father knows what you need before you ask him. This is how you are to pray: Our Father in heaven, hallowed be your name, your kingdom come, your will be done, on earth as in heaven.*

*Give us today our daily bread; and forgive us
our debts, as we forgive our debtors; and do not
subject us to the final test, but deliver us from the
evil one."*

Matthew 6: 5-13 (NAB)

When we reflect on the words Jesus taught us, we learn the power of this prayer. Since most of us learn the Lord's Prayer at an early age, many of us don't take time to reflect on it and study it as an adult. With those words, Jesus is teaching us that "if we forgive others their transgressions, our Heavenly Father will forgive us. If we do not forgive others, neither will our Father forgive our transgressions." Matthew 6:14-15 (NAB)

Someone once said, "What we usually pray to God for is not that His will be done, but that He approves ours."[1]

I believe you do not have to attend church to pray, but you might want to attend church to experience forgiveness. In John's Gospel, Jesus gave the church the power to forgive sin:

*(Jesus) said to them again, "Peace be with you.
As the Father has sent me, so I send you." And
when he had said this, he breathed on them and
said to them, "Receive the Holy Spirit whose sins
you forgive are forgiven them, and whose sins
you retain are retained."*

John 20:21-23 (NAB)

"It's easy to forgive, but forgetting takes a long time." Willie Nelson[2]

Forgive and forget. Do you know that, as Christians, each of us has that same power to forgive and retain sins against us? Let me explain: when someone wrongs you, and then asks for forgiveness, you have the power to forgive them. And when you forgive that person, you give them a blessing. But if you can forget their offense against you, then you give yourself a blessing. Forgive and forget; if not, then you will forgive and retain.

After I was ordained a deacon in the Catholic Church, I was given the privilege to preach the gospel at mass. My parents, who were recently retired, would come to mass to hear their son preach. I believe they saw in their son someone who reflected back to them "my father's wisdom and my mother's love" as well as my own love for the gospel. After that, my parents attended mass regularly for the rest of their lives. My dad, being a businessman and very good at handling money, became one of the "money counters" at his parish.

You were right, Dad. "You don't have to go to Cleveland to have fun" and "You don't have to go to church to pray." Yet when we attend church, we are with fellow believers who help support our own faith and help us to realize that we are not alone in our belief.

9
"The Blind Leading The Blind"

Jesus said these words two thousand years ago, but the first time I heard them was when my dad said them in comment to my trying to break in a new stock boy at our grocery store. Again, I took no offense because I thought it was another one of my dad's funny sayings that also conveyed truth.

When I think of spiritual direction and the church, I hope that it is not like the blind leading the blind, but rather the enlightened leading the unenlightened from darkness into light. The origin of the word "church" comes from the Latin word *ecclesia*, which derives from *ek* meaning "out"; and *kahic*, meaning "called," in Greek. In other words, the church is the people of God, "called out" of the darkness into the light.

When I was living in Coronado, California, my daughter Gina and I attended a Christology class given by Fr. Ron Perchance, a professor at the University of San Diego. I will never forget something surprising that he said: "Jesus did not come to start the Roman Catholic Church." He said the word "church," or *ecclesia*, is only mentioned twice in the scriptures. Rather, Jesus mentions the "Kingdom" of God many times. I believe he said the word "Kingdom" appears some thirty plus times in the New Testament. I do believe that Jesus came to reveal the "Kingdom of God," to show us what heaven is like and also to know God...

> *"From that time on, Jesus began to preach and say, "Repent, for the Kingdom of Heaven is at hand."*
>
> *Matthew 4:17 (NAB)*

and...

> *"Then the righteous will shine like the sun in the Kingdom of their Father. Whoever has ears ought to hear."*
>
> *Matthew 13:43 (NAB)*

He was in fact calling God's people to come out of the darkness and into the light.

You don't have to go to church to pray, but if you want a greater experience of God, Jesus Christ, and the Holy Spirit, you might want to join together with other believers to share your faith. I once used the analogy that going to church was like downloading a new program into your computer. When the installation is complete, you are instructed to restart your computer. Much like when you go to church, you are downloading scriptures, prayers, homilies (or sermons), thanksgiving, praise, worship, fellowship, and in some cases, the Eucharist into your computer. All of this leads to a new start. You are then "restarted" and ready to leave that church with renewed and refreshed faith. You are better equipped to offer your faith and love to a world that sorely needs it.

Jesus said, "The Sabbath was made for man, not man for the Sabbath" Mark 2:27b (NAB). That is why I don't believe Sunday's mass or any other feast day mass should be an "obligation," as it is in my Church; at least so much so that it is considered a sin if you miss mass without good reason. I do believe attending mass should be called an "opportunity" instead of an "obligation." It is an opportunity to honor and praise God and to give thanks to Him. I remember Fr. Dominic Valentino once said during mass, "If you are only here because Sunday mass is an obligation, I give you dispensation, you don't have to be here. You should be here out of gratitude. You should be here to give God thanks and praise. On the other hand, if you have nothing to be thankful for... stay home." So, whether you call it worship, fellowship, Eucharist, or Sabbath, you don't have to go to church to pray, but why deprive yourself of His grace?

Another thing I learned from Fr. Valentino was the way he made the sign of the cross for his private prayer. He would say, "In the name of the Father who created me, and of the Son who redeemed me, and the Holy Spirit who inspires me. Amen." This little prayer with the sign of the cross sums up the theology of the Trinity, one in which we Christians believe.

I once heard this story about a man who had not gone to church in some time, and so his pastor paid him a visit. The man offered his pastor a cup of coffee, and they sat in front of the fireplace. As they were discussing the reasons why the man did not attend church, the fire grew warm and cozy. As they sat there staring at the fire, it sparked, and an ember fell away from the fire. As they continued to watch, the ember began to fade and then it went out altogether. Both men paused and watched the ember go out. Then the man told his pastor, I'll see you on Sunday.

Don't let your faith burn out.

10
"Grazie A Dio"

When my siblings and I were young, we were taught to thank God at the end of each meal, as well as saying the blessing before meals. My grandfather, named Adario Vivio, known to us as "Nonno," used to slap the table edge and say, *"Grazie a Dio"* (Thank God), when he finished dinner. So, when we were finished eating, in addition to asking if we could be excused from the dining table, we would say, *"Grazie a Dio,"* when we got up from the table.

When I use the word "Eucharist," when talking about the Roman Catholic Mass, I am referring to the Communion that we receive at mass. I am using a word from the ancient Greek meaning "Thanksgiving." We use the word *Eucharist* interchangeably for the entire mass and for Communion. The mass is our time to offer thanksgiving, and Jesus' presence in the Communion that we receive, is that for which we are thankful. *Grazie a Dio!*

As I was writing the previous chapter about church, I was thinking about this whole idea of church and who we are as the church. Then I attended mass that particular Sunday, and as it happened, it was the Feast of Corpus Christi, that is, the Feast of the Body and Blood of Jesus Christ. In the Roman Catholic tradition, we have long revered the Eucharist, the consecrated bread and wine transubstantiated into the Body and Blood of Christ. This is a tradition carried forward from the earliest days of the church and our understanding of the Gospel of Christ.

> *"While they were eating, Jesus took bread, said the blessing, broke it, and giving it to his disciples said, "Take and eat; this is my body. Then he took a cup, gave thanks, and gave it to them, saying, "Drink from it, all of you, for this is my blood of the covenant, which will be shed on behalf of many for the forgiveness of sins."*
>
> *Matthew 26:26-28 (NAB)*

Many years ago, at my ordination retreat, our bishop, James Raush, came to visit our retreat, and he gave us a lesson on the proper distribution of Communion (the Eucharist) at mass. The distribution of the Eucharist is a solemn moment in the mass, when the minister takes the host and holds it up for the communicant to see and adore before receiving it. Bishop Raush said that we should not rush or make this moment too informal. We should simply hold the host and say, "the Body of Christ." He said, "As you, the minister, make that declaration, you are staring at the host and looking at the same time at the recipient and making the statement 'the Body of Christ.' In doing so, you are acknowledging the presence of our Lord in both the host and the person who is about to receive it."

In other words, both the host and the person are the Body of Christ, and when the recipient simply says, "Amen," which means "I believe" or "I agree" or "I accept," he or she acknowledges that truth.

As I was remembering Bishop Rausch and his teaching at the mass for the Feast of Corpus Christi, the time came for Communion. As I watched the people come forward to receive the Eucharist, my eyes filled with tears as I realized this was "Corpus Christi," the Body and Blood of Christ.

I witnessed a single mother with three small children struggling to share her faith with her children, and I saw that the Body of Christ is hopeful but unsure about her future.

I saw a middle-aged man, recently laid off from his job, coming to the Eucharist with sad eyes, and I saw the Body of Christ fearful and feeling lost.

I saw an old man barely able to walk down the aisle and with trembling hands and adoring eyes look at the host with tremendous faith, and I saw the Body of Christ is sometimes weak and frail.

I saw a young girl of the age of seven, who recently received her first Communion, come forth with eyes as wide as saucers and a smile that radiated throughout the church, and I saw that the Body of Christ is young and filled with love and joy.

And, I reflected on what St. Augustine said, that "we become what we eat."[1] Therefore, in that moment, we become the Body of Christ. My eyes filled with tears as I witnessed the Body of Christ as we receive it, sometimes bent and broken, sometimes weak and sinful, sometimes fearful, and sometimes joyful.

I was moved as I realized: "Yes, this is the Body of Christ. *Grazie a Dio!*"

11

"The Eleventh Commandment...Don't Get Caught"

My dad would say this when he wanted to make a point about getting caught when doing something wrong. Whether you were caught in a lie, or a man was caught cheating on his wife or his taxes, or a politician was caught in a corruption scandal, my dad would respond with this statement as a humorous way of teaching a lesson. Others might have said, "If you can't do the time, don't do the crime." My dad's saying was, "Always do the right thing: tell the truth; be reliable; don't cheat; be an honorable person. But if you can't, just remember the eleventh commandment... Don't get caught!" My dad knew that there was no eleventh commandment, but he also knew that you will always get caught.

One day in high school, my buddies and I decided not to go to school one fine autumn day; so we played hooky. We spent the day at the old swimming hole, drank sodas, smoked cigarettes, and bragged about our imagined exploits with girls. After a fun day in the sun we went home for supper. After the meal, I went down to the basement family room to watch TV with my dad. He said, "I got a call from your school today," which surprised me because my parents were never home during the day as they were always working at our grocery store. I guess some enterprising secretary at school must have researched my file and found my parents' phone number at the store. After I recovered from his initial statement, I said, "Oh yeah, what did they want?" He said, "They told me that you missed school today, and that you and your friends decided to play hooky." What could I say? I was busted. I was silent for a moment, and my dad said, "You forgot the eleventh commandment. Don't get caught." Well, that lightened the moment for me and my dad and allowed us to go on to discuss why I did not like school. We discussed how I saw my future and my plans for it. This was one of those incidents in a young man's life when father and son could share thoughts, feelings, and experiences, such that I will never forget. I am so grateful for having those moments when my dad and I were alone and he would share his stories and wisdom.

Many young men have not had such experiences with their fathers. Men of my generation did not experience their fathers as I did, because many of those fathers never told their sons that they loved them. This is sad on many levels, but I ran into it often when I taught classes to those inquiring into entering the Catholic Church. I would teach about Jesus Christ, the Holy Spirit, and the loving Father, who so loved the world that he sent his only Son. Once in a while a man would come up to me and say that he was having a hard time relating to a loving father, because his own father was not very loving, and in some cases, may have even been abusive. I would try to be aware of this when I spoke of our Heavenly Father as a God of love. In the time of Christ, people would ask him to show them the Father and to tell them what he was like.

> *"Have I been with you for so long a time and you*
> *still do not know me, Philip? Whoever has seen*
> *me has seen the Father. How can you say, 'Show*
> *us the Father'? Do you not believe that I am in the*
> *Father and the Father is in me? The words that*
> *I speak to you I do not speak on my own. The*
> *Father who dwells in me is doing his works."*
>
> *John 14:9-10 (NAB)*

Jesus came among us to show us what the Father is like, and to show us what the kingdom of God was like. As followers of Christ, we are to do the same, by sharing the Good News with others.

I believe to know him is to love him, and the best way to know him is to study the scriptures and read what Jesus and his first followers did and preached. All of the early disciples were willing to put their lives on the line for what they believed.

> *"No one has greater love than this, to lay down*
> *one's life for one's friends."*
>
> *John 15:13 (NAB)*

Many men and woman fear their fathers; many more fear our Heavenly Father, because they never knew him.

> *"I have told you this so that you may not fall*
> *away. They will expel you from the synagogues;*

*in fact, the hour is coming when everyone who
kills you will think he is offering worship to God.
They will do this because they have not known
either the Father or me."*

John 16-1-3 (NAB)

To know him is to love him. To love him is to follow
him and spread his love.

*"I give you a new commandment: love one
another. As I have loved you, so you also should
love one another. This is how all will know that
you are my disciples, if you have love for one
another."*

John 13:34-35 (NAB)

Who am I? I am who I am... I believe you should get to
know yourself better, put aside false humility, and come
to know who you really are. Try going to the scriptures
again and think of the love that the Father has lavished
on us through His Son.

*"See what love the Father has bestowed on us
that we may be called the children of God. Yet so
we are. The reason the world does not know us is
that it did not know him. Beloved, we are God's
children now; what we shall be has not yet been
revealed. We do know that when it is revealed we
shall be like him, for we shall see him as he is."*

I John 3:1-2 (NAB)

I have often thought about this question, and I have asked myself, "Who am I?" After some contemplation, I can now confidently say who I am. I am a son of God; I am husband, I am father, I am grandfather, I am brother, I am friend; I am a deacon, a minister, a preacher, a teacher, a writer, and a purveyor of wisdom and truth.

Think about it: who are you? How would you answer the question? Who do you say you are? And remember the eleventh commandment, "Don't get caught..." not being what you have chosen to be. Also, when reflecting on who you are, remember that you are not just what others say you are. You are not merely what you do...you are who you are. As a christian you are a child of God. You are a human being, not a human doing. What are you being?

Complete this statement: *"I am..."*

12
"He Ain't Feeling No Pain"

My dad would sometimes stand looking out of the front window of his grocery store on a payday, or the day the "eagle flew over" (meaning the day the government checks came in the mail). Sometimes my dad would see some guy walking down the street who was really high on something—drugs, alcohol, or both. It was comical to watch these guys walk along and try to negotiate the broken sidewalk or the curb. These guys would be stepping high and very carefully, and my dad would say, "He ain't feeling no pain." meaning this guy was so high, so numb that he really felt no pain. For now...

If you are high on something, or if you are holding so much of your feelings back in life so you don't feel any pain, you should take your pulse to be sure you're still alive. Life is about growth and change. And growth and change can be painful. The pain stops when life stops. For the Christian there is suffering and then Glory.

"Was it not necessary that the Messiah should suffer these things and enter into his glory?"

Luke 24:26 (NAB)

I have many fond memories of my parents' grocery store, as I am sure my family did as well. One memory that may have been very painful for my parents and others, however, was in April of 1968. Their grocery store was located in a working-class neighborhood of mixed ethnic groups, yet everyone got along very well despite the racial conflicts of the 1960s. However, on April 4, 1968, Dr. Martin Luther King Jr. was assassinated. Following that tragic day, many African American neighborhoods exploded in anger and frustration. Many of the people took it personally, as if their own family member had been assassinated, as many truly felt he was one of their family members. If you lived or studied the history of this time, you know that "race riots" broke out across the nation in response to his death. In some places, it was reported that outside instigators, possibly communists, were stirring up anger and encouraging the people to burn and destroy the "white-owned" businesses in their neighborhoods. The sad reality was that this caused many businesses in those neighborhoods to close and not reopen ever again. This caused many poor people— mothers and grandmothers, without automobiles or other transportation—to have to travel by streetcar or bus to another neighborhood to buy groceries and other important supplies for their families.

Coincidentally, our neighborhood remained fairly calm; as I said, most folks there got along very well. My dad had a very good relationship with our neighbors. He had always taught us kids from the time that we were very young to respect all people regardless of their race or ethnicity. After all, isn't that what America was all about? Also, he told stories of the nasty remarks and prejudices that he and his family had to endure as Italian immigrants.

The people in that neighborhood around their food market loved and respected my parents. My parents were vital members of the community. My dad was a big help to those who were down financially or in need of a helping hand. I saw him pay the rent, gas and electric bills for people, or let families run a food bill until they found work again or when the strike against the steel mill was over. I guess it was because of my parents' acts of kindness and respect for others that the people held them in such high esteem. But then one day a customer and friend of my dad stopped by the store. He told him that there were outside agitators trying to get the people in that neighborhood to riot and burn out my parents' store. My dad's friend said that he and others argued against them, but still it was better to be safe than sorry. So this friend suggested that my dad close the store early and get out of town with the family, so that no one would get hurt. My parents did as they suggested, and closed the store for a few days. The disturbances finally quieted down, and my parents' store was never vandalized. I guess calmer heads prevailed. It seemed things were never the same after that incident, and since my parents could not sell the store, which was now located in such a volatile neighborhood, they decided to just close the store and board it up like so many other inner-city businesses. The story has a happy ending, as my parents opened another business and eventually found their way to the southwest, where they enjoyed some of the best years of their life in Phoenix, Arizona.

Think of some of the painful events in your life. How many of these events are you grateful for today? Because thanks to them you are changed, and you grew into the person you are today. It has been said that "God's greatest gifts are not 'things,' but 'opportunities.'"[1]

I once attended a seminar on male spirituality given by Fr. Richard Rohr (OFM) [2], who taught that growth is found in the dirt, mire, and mud of life. He said, "Life is found in facing fear and death. It's not found in the pleasant and comfortable. When you can't fix it, you can't control it, and you don't even understand it. There in your helplessness you encounter God."

Henri Nouwen said, "God comes to you disguised as your life."[3]

I once saw a great bumper sticker that read:

"Business is Great!
People are Terrific!
Life is Wonderful!"[4]

It's true, "Attitude is everything." In our modern world of "bumper sticker" theology and "sound bite" philosophies, that particular bumper sticker has stayed with me and resonated with me for the last ten years. I am not a Pollyanna, but a pragmatist. It is true. *Attitude IS everything!*

For example...

"Business is terrific!"

Always? Yes. Why? Because business, even in a down cycle, is an important means of life. Like life, it will inevitably come back and thrive. And we are fortunate to be a part of the business of life, whether you are a CEO of a large corporation, a small entrepreneur, or in a new-hire, entry-level position. Business, all business, gives us our living and prosperity. And if one business is down, another is thriving.

"People are great!"

You know they are. I know that there are many flawed individuals, but on the whole when you think about it, men and woman were created in God's image (Genesis 1:27). Therefore, we have the potential to be great. We can procreate, increase, multiply, create, invent, fly, and even travel in space. But our potential to love is our greatest gift from the Creator, who is love.

"Life is wonderful!"

Is it not? Look at your life, your abilities, your spouse, your children, and your opportunities. Sure, you could dwell on the shortcomings or failures. But why? This wonderful life of yours is very short. Why waste time worrying, complaining, and wishing it were otherwise? Be wise and look at what God has given you. Bloom where you are planted, and like the old Army poster used to say, "Be all that you can be."

Like I said, I am not a Pollyanna, I am a pragmatist. Your life will be better spent living it to the fullest than sitting around complaining about what might have been. I know that I tend to be optimistic and positive thinking.

This comes from my many years in the sales profession and the training I have been given. I have attended many sales seminars and I have heard many motivational speakers. One of my favorite speakers was Zig Ziegler. Of all that he has said and written, the one thing that stands out most is, "We all need a daily checkup from the neck up to avoid stinkin' thinkin', which ultimately leads to hardening of the attitudes."[5]

In trying to avoid negativity or negative talk, many managers and salespeople address problems as a difficulty, a challenge, or a situation. Often these problems should be viewed as opportunities—opportunities for growth. Once, a coworker of mine was having problems with a product and a difficult customer. In the end, all went well, and everyone was happy. I told my coworker then, "See, everything usually works out for the best." After I thought about that statement, I restated it to my coworker, saying, "You know what? Things always work out for the best, but we are just not always aware of it." So, whether you call them problems, situations, or challenges, they all add to our experience of life. If you are not feeling any pain, remember: "No pain, no gain."

The sum of your years is not who you are. But they prepare you to be who you choose to be.

13
"Salute!"

"God looked at everything he had made, and he found it very good..."

Gen. 1:31a (NAB)

The character of Alonzo Harris, played by Denzel Washington in the movie *Training Day*, would say, "It's all good!"[1]

A Jewish celebrant might say, *"Mazel Tov!'*

A Hispanic enthusiast might say, *"Mucho Gusto!"*

But Vic Vivio would have said, *"SAAA-LUTE!"* with emphasis on the first syllable of the Italian word "salute," which means, "To your health." or "Cheers!"

My dad used the word "salute" to express a positive reaction to many things, besides using it as a toast when sharing a drink—but always when sharing a drink.

A good report card. *"SAAA-LUTE!"*

An engagement announcement. *"SAAA-LUTE!"*

A birth announcement. *"SAAA-LUTE!"*

Purchase a new house. *"SAAA-LUTE!"*

Any good news you share. *"SAAA-LUTE!"*

The exclamation *salute* was so much associated with my dad that he even ordered a vanity license plate for his car that read "SAL-UTE".

He used the word as a way of saying, "Thank God." It was a word that conveyed a good attitude and gratitude. What a great way to live—remember, Attitude is everything. But what I learned from my dad was to have gratitude for everything. Taken together, we should live with an attitude of gratitude.

There is a story I once heard about two officials standing in an empty synagogue. They decided to approach the area around the Torah to pray. In the back of the room, standing in the shadows, was a janitor who watched the officials praying. He decided to join them. The first official looked up toward heaven, hands spread apart, and said, "Oh merciful God, have mercy on me. I know I am nothing." The second official also looked up and prayed, "Oh merciful God, have mercy on me. I know I am nothing." So the janitor was impressed, and he too prayed aloud, "Oh merciful God, have mercy on me. I know I am nothing." The first official looked at the janitor and then nudged the other official and said, "Look who thinks he's a nothing."

> *He then addressed this parable to those who were convinced of their own righteousness and despised everyone else. "Two people went up to the temple area to pray; one was a Pharisee and the other was a tax collector. The Pharisee took up his position and spoke this prayer to himself, 'O God, I thank you that I am not like the rest of humanity--greedy, dishonest, adulterous--or even like this tax collector. I fast twice a week, and I pay tithes on my whole income.' But the tax*

*collector stood off at a distance and would not
even raise his eyes to heaven but beat his breast
and prayed, 'O God, be merciful to me a sinner.'
I tell you, the latter went home justified, not the
former; for everyone who exalts himself will be
humbled, and the one who humbles himself will
be exalted."*

Luke 18: 9-14 (NAB)

When we read the above verses in Luke 18, we need
to ask some questions. Who is proud? Who is humble?
Who went away justified before the Lord? Also, how do
you mean what you say? Remember, it is not just what
you say, but how you say it. When you pray, do you have
that sense of awe when speaking to the Almighty? And
still, if you feel special in your relationship with God,
that's okay...you are special! You are just no more special
than anyone else. As Christians, we each have a special
relationship with God. Each of us is His beloved.

Did you ever wonder why the disciple John referred to
himself as the "beloved disciple"? I once had a spiritual
director who had the theory that John used the term
"beloved" to describe what he knew to be true—that he
was loved by the Lord Jesus. Not that he was more loved
than any other, or to the exclusion of all others, but that
he was aware of Jesus' tremendous love for him, and for
His people. He knew that he was truly loved, the beloved
disciple of Jesus.

All of us, who study the gospel and commune with
God in prayer, and offer praise and worship to him,

should come to the same conclusion, that you are loved, you are his *beloved.*

Sometime when you are at prayer, try to put aside all of the noise and distractions of our selfish and violent world. Put aside the world that tries to keep us off guard and wants our attention to the exclusion of all else. Try as much as possible to be at peace and listen to that still small voice within us that says, "You are my *beloved*...on you my favor rests." Jesus did, John the Apostle did, and so can you.

Our day-to-day business certainly is a distraction. Keep in mind the words of Jesus:

> *"Martha, Martha, you are anxious and worried about many things. There is need of only one thing. Mary has chosen the better part and it will not be taken from her."*
>
> *Luke 10:41-42 (NAB)*

Jesus is telling us only one "thing" is needed, and it is our choice. That "thing" is the Word of God, and our relationship with Him. Learn to settle yourself, learn to listen, and you too shall have the better part.

You say that you want a deep communion with God. I love this excerpt from *With Burning Hearts: A Meditation on the Eucharistic Life,* by Henri J. M. Nouwen:

> *"God says he wants communion with you. God says he wants a deep relationship with you. God says; see how much I love you? I was born among you as an infant, to be dependent upon you for food and nurturing and fondling and*

love. I was a little boy among you who needed guidance and protection and advice. I was a young man among you, where I experienced community, love, laughter, disappointment, sorrow, and loss. I was tried as a criminal and was scourged, and nailed to a cross for your sins. I was raised from the dead to show you my tremendous love for you, and to promise you eternal life... This is my love for you. Now, after all this, I ask you...Do you love me? Do you love me? Do you love me?"[2]

And God looked at everything that he created and said, "It is good."

"God looked at everything he had made, and he found it very good..."

Gen. 1:31a (NAB)

I have a little sign on the wall of my cabin that reads: "It's a wonderful life." Each day I read it and I remember,

IT'S ALL GOOD...SALUTE!

14
"Alzarsi—A Wake-Up Call"

My dad was born June 9, 1915, the same year as his favorite singer, Frank Sinatra. My dad was baptized with the name of Vittorio Emanuele Vivio. He was named after the king of Italy at the time, Vittorio Emanuele III. His father told him that when the king died, he would be the next king. But as happened to millions of immigrants at that time in our history, hospitals and government officials changed chosen and family names in order to Americanize them. So my father's name became Victor Emanuel Vivio.

My dad would tell a story of how his father, my *nonno* (meaning "grandfather") Adario Vivio, would call to him to wake him up in the morning. He would say *"Alzarsi,"* which means "get up" or "wake up" in Italian. We liked the way my dad told this story using Nonno's Italian accent, so as I go on with the story, I will use my Nonno's dialect and my dad's imitation of his father to tell the story like my dad did.

My nonno pronounced *"Alzarsi"* as *"Aleetzada,"* and the name Victor as *"Vee-toh."* My nonno would call up to my dad from downstairs, "Vee-toh, Vee-toh, Vee-toh," until my dad finally answered, "What?" *"Aleetzada"*, Nonno would say. And then my dad, like a lot of young men who stayed out too late the night before, would fall back to sleep. A little later came that haunting call form downstairs, "Vee-toh, Vee-toh, Vee-toh," until my dad finally answered, "What?" "*Aleetzada!*" Nonno answered, and my dad would call out, "Okay." and then fall asleep again. Until later he heard it again, "Vee-toh, Vee-toh, Vee-toh." We had such fun listening to my dad imitate his father when he told this story.

Sometimes when my dad would catch one of us kids not paying attention to what we were doing, or "sleeping at the switch," my dad would say to us, "*Aleetzada!*" We knew what he meant.

Today we would call that a wake-up call, something each of us needs from time to time. I include "*alzarsi*" here because many people go through life sleepwalking. Many are asleep at the switch and don't know it. Jesus promises to send believers an advocate. The Spirit of Truth, who guides us to all truth. Many of us, I'm afraid, are not aware of the Holy Spirit at work in our lives. Either we don't take Jesus at His Word or we don't believe we are worthy. I think that the latter is true. And yet, if we believe that we are not worth it, we make a mockery of Jesus Christ and his Father who sent him.

> *For God so loved the world that he gave his only*
> *Son so that everyone who believes in him might*
> *not perish but might have eternal life.*
>
> *John 3:16 (NAB)*

Many of us go through life not aware of our potential, and even more of us are unaware of the potential of the Holy Spirit in our lives. I have over the years taken an interest in "spiritual direction." I have studied it. I have practiced it, and I have come to the conclusion that the greatest need in the Church is not more study, knowledge, and theology, not more social and special needs programs, but better spiritual direction. People really want and need direction in their spiritual lives. One antidote making light of Moses that I always enjoyed, asked the question, "Why did it take forty years for the Israelites to find their way from Egypt to the Promised Land?" The answer, "Because Moses was a real man, and real men don't ask for directions."

Well, most of us don't ask for spiritual direction either! When I first heard the term "spiritual direction," I shunned the idea. I thought that it meant that you went to a priest, kind of like going to confession, and the priest would scrutinize your spiritual life (i.e., did you say your prayers every day, did you go to church every Sunday, and just what did you believe?). Well, I found out that is *not* what spiritual direction is all about. What spiritual direction means is that you and the person you choose (male or female) walk your spiritual path together. The spiritual director, more than anything, points out along the way your own encounter with God in your life, and how the promises of the Christ are coming alive on your journey. You learn how the Holy Spirit is there for you and how the Spirit can help you through difficult experiences and making decisions if you but trust him. Through spiritual direction you learn to trust the Holy Spirit and look for his action in your life.

"But if you are guided by the Spirit, you are not under the law."

Gal.5:18 (NAB)

Alzarsi! Get up, wake up! We need a wake-up call. Not to "wake up and smell the coffee," nor to just "stop and smell the roses," but to come to the awareness of the Holy Spirit and the gift of God that it is there for all believers.

"The Kingdom of God is at hand…"

Mark 1:15 (NAB)

Turn inward and seek the kingdom within you…once done, look for others to wake up and share the Good News with them. ALZARSI!

*"Blessed are those servants whom the master finds vigilant [or **awake**, emphasis mine] on his arrival."*

Luke 12:37 (NAB)

15
"Don't Worry, Be Happy"

"The Glory of God is a human being fully alive."

St. Irenaeus[1]

I guess I have always been a "big picture" guy. Even as a child I would think way ahead. As soon as we finished celebrating my birthday in April, I would start planning and looking forward to Christmas. When summer vacation ended and the school year began in September, I would mark the calendar for the last day of school. It has been like this with everything. I am always planning and looking ahead.

My dad would say, "You're wishing your life away." And my mom would tell me, "Oh, you worry too much." But I disagreed because I was not worrying or wishing my life away; I saw it as preparing and planning ahead. Later in life I took a Dale Carnegie course on public speaking and getting along with people.[2] One of the weekly lessons had to do with worrying. We studied a book titled *How to Stop Worrying and Start Living*.[3] There were many stories of individuals who overcame obstacles in life by dealing with them and not worrying. One story I remember was about the billionaire named J. Paul Getty. Carnegie related how Getty dealt with worry. Carnegie wrote, "When he [Getty] would enter into a new business or project, he would plan out everything, even the possibility of failure. And then he would think of what he would do if in fact he did experience failure. He would decide what he would do and how he would move on, and knowing how he would survive, he would accept that possible outcome. He then said, he would work very hard to make sure that outcome would never happen."[4]

When I read the above statement, I realized that is what I have always done. I told my mom, "See, I am not a worrier, I'm a planner." I don't worry. I just try to be happy. I really have learned from my parents to live my life to the fullest without worrying about the future.

I think my wife and my sister in-law had to get used to my parents' attitude about life. If one of them was concerned about something, say a sick child or an unpaid bill, or what to do about thus and such, my mom would usually say, "Oh don't worry, things will be all right," or "Everything will work out fine." I think they thought that my mom was a bit cavalier or not caring enough. But really she did care, she just did not want to seem overly concerned and cause greater angst for the younger women. Besides, as they say these days, both moms and dads have "been there and done that."

As I grow older, I have the typical aches and pains that come with age. And as I have had more and more health problems after I recently retired, I ask myself, "What If I only have five years left to live? What would I do? Just what would I do? I have enough money to travel, to enjoy my life doing whatever I want to do. So, just what would I want to do?" I guess we all have asked ourselves that or similar questions in moments of introspection. To tell the truth, my answer to that question is, "I am already doing exactly what I want to do...EXACTLY." I am very happy with where I am at this time of my life...my life as it is...is as it should be.

Once I asked some friends that I often meet for breakfast, "What would you do if your doctor told you that you only had six months to live?" One friend said he'd quit his job and travel. One said he would "live it up" and max out his credit cards. Another said that he would start smoking again. After the laughter, they settled down and spoke of more serious activities, such as: I would go back to church again. I would start to read the Bible. I would start to pray again. I would be kinder, I would be more loving to my wife and kids, I would commit random acts of kindness and be more loving to everyone, etc. And then I asked them to consider this question: "Who says that you have six months to live?"

My dad used to say, "When you are dead, you are dead a long time." So make the most of the time God has given you, and stop worrying and start living.

"Look at the birds in the sky; they do not sow or reap, they gather nothing into barns, yet your heavenly Father feeds them. Are not you more important than they? Can any of you by worrying add a single moment to your life-span? Why are you anxious about clothes? Learn from the way the wild flowers grow. They do not work or spin.

But I tell you that not even Solomon in all his splendor was clothed like one of them."

Matthew 6:26-29 (NAB)

Here's something I discovered about King Solomon. A researcher found a recipe from a cookbook that was found in King Solomon's ruins: "30m. flour, 60m. meal, 10 fat oxen, 20 free gazelles, roebucks, and fattened fowl." Also found were golden plates, cups, and a gold plated ivory throne. Wow. Solomon could throw a party.

As a warrior; he never lost a battle. He had 1,400 war chariots and 12,000 horses. As for wisdom, he was considered the wisest of all men. He composed over 3,000 proverbs and wrote 1,500 poems. "But I tell you that not even Solomon in all his splendor was clothed like one of them." Matthew 6:29 (NAB)

Fear is useless; what is needed is trust.

Or as Jesus would say, "Do not be afraid; just have faith."

Mark 5:36 (NAB)

Christians must try to remain close to the Lord at all times. All we need to do is trust him and constantly communicate with him through prayer.

O Lord, Please show me the way.
Even when I am not looking....

16
"Abbondanza!"

"I came so that they might have life and have it more abundantly."

John 10:10b (NAB)

"My sheep hear my voice; I know them, and they follow me. I give them eternal life, and they shall never perish. No one can take them out of my hand."

John 10:27, 28 (NAB)

Abundant life...Eternal life. As Christians, what more could you ask for? What more could you want?

I must say as I reflect back on my life, I know that I have had an abundant one. When I was five years old my parents bought a grocery store. Have you ever heard the saying, "It's like being a kid in a candy store"? Well, I lived that saying. I was given whatever I wanted in the store, all I had to do was ask. This is also how my dad taught me the lesson, "Be careful what you ask for, you just might get it." You might have thought my brother Ed, my sister Vivian, and I were spoiled. I guess maybe in some ways, we were. But our parents knew that they had good children and that we would be working hard around the store to help them run their new business, so they would often indulge us. When our family opened the store, and when we also moved into the apartment above it, we three kids truly lived like "kids in a candy store." Whatever we wanted or asked for...we got. Yes, it sounds like we were spoiled children, all right. But my dad, being a wise man, never missed a chance to teach a life lesson. After a few days of bingeing on candies, cakes, ice cream, cookies, Popsicles, and fruit, our faces began to turn various shades of green, and in between our vomiting and diarrhea, we would lay about in the back room of the store moaning about our bellyaches. Then my dad would teasingly stick his head in the door and ask if we wanted any more candy. We would groan, "No, my belly aches." A short time later he would pop in again to ask if we wanted some ice cream or Popsicles, and we would give the same groan in response. Here, my mom and dad taught us to be careful what we asked for, and to ask responsibly. And having learned that lesson well, we, from that time on, knew what to ask for and how to ask for it; we usually got what we wanted.

My parents sold a popular pizza in the store by Mama Celeste, and I remember the Mama Celeste TV commercials. There was a pleasant-looking Italian grandmother with gray hair and glasses, and she would describe one of her pizzas with this wonderful Italian word, *"Abbondanza,"* which means "abundance." This pizza was loaded with everything, and just to look at it, one word came to mind: *"Abbondanza!"*

I think of that word to help me better understand Jesus Christ, for example, in John's Gospel, where Jesus said, "I came so that they might have life and have it more abundantly." John 10:10*b* (NAB)

I believe that Christians can live the abundant life now. I am not talking about having lots of money, fancy clothes, new cars, properties, expensive homes, or even enough food to gorge yourself like I had when I was a kid in the grocery store. I am saying that when you believe, and walk in the Lord, that you have everything you want, and need nothing.

> *"The LORD is my shepherd; there is nothing I lack (**want**—emphasis mine)."*
>
> *Psalm 23:1 (NAB)*

It is wanting that creates need; want nothing, need nothing. Bless what shows up in your life. Now you are living the abundant life. And the Word of God, rich as it is, will provide you with all that you will ever need, and you will abide in his love all of your days.

> *"Instead, seek his Kingdom, and these other things will be given you besides."*
>
> *Luke 12:31 (NAB)*

You may be happy with what you have, or happy with what you get. Either way, there is joy. There is abundance. You are blessed.

17
"Old-Timer's Disease"

"As I approach the prime of my life
I find I have the time of my life
Learning to enjoy at my leisure
All the simple pleasures
And so I happily concede
This is all I ask.
This is all I need."

(Lyrics made famous by Tony Bennett)[1]

I first heard that song by Nat Cole when I was eighteen years old, then later it was a big hit by Tony Bennett. I am sixty-five years old, and as I write this book, I find the words of that song to be truer for me than ever. As I look back over my life, I think more and more about "my father's wisdom and my mothers' love," and their words echo in my mind more frequently.

On aging, my dad used to say, "If I knew I was going to live this long, I would have taken better care of myself." My dad lived until he was eighty-one years of age. When his health began to fail, he would say, "Have your fun while you're young." I remember when my dad retired at the age of sixty-five and we discussed the notion of growing older. I had just turned forty, and I questioned my dad, "Who would want to live until age ninety-five?" And Dad answered, "A ninety-four-year-old."

My dad also liked to quote his favorite sports hero, the late great heavyweight boxing champion Joe Louis, who once said, "Everybody wants to go to heaven, but nobody wants to die to get there."[2]

Wisdom is one of the benefits that come with age. It is true for many, but not for all. By that I mean that you gain wisdom when you learn from your mistakes and the mistakes of others. I wrote earlier that ever since I can remember, I tried to learn from others' mistakes and not to repeat them in my life. As I grow older, I also try to learn from others' successes and the positive aspects of their lives and try to emulate them as well. It's like the story I once heard about a young bull being yoked together with an old bull.

A deacon friend of mine once visited Jerusalem, Israel, for a vacation and retreat. He was also in the process of continuing his studies as a deacon and an educator at the time. He told me that one day he was sitting in the shade of an olive tree in the garden at Gethsemane. He was reading scripture, and upon looking up he saw a farmer in the distance training a yoke of oxen. By that he meant the farmer had a young bull yoked with an old bull. The young bull did not want to be yoked at all. He was restless and would not walk in a straight line. But the old bull was steadfast and strong and helped the farmer train the young bull. After several tries and struggles, the young bull finally began to come around. He began to walk straight and pull his share of the load. My friend said that in that moment, the scripture

passage that Jesus taught about taking his yoke upon
our shoulders became crystal clear to him.

"Come to me, all you who labor and are
burdened, and I will give you rest. Take my yoke
upon you and learn from me, for I am meek and
humble of heart; and you will find rest for your
selves. For my yoke is easy, and my burden
light."

Matthew 11: 28-30 (NAB)

The first disciples of Jesus understood this example
very well; it was common knowledge how to train a yoke
of oxen. Every time I read this scripture passage, I think
of my friend's experience and his watching a yoke of oxen
being trained. When you look at this passage, it is quite
beautiful: Jesus is inviting us to intimacy with him. He
knows we are tired and weary, and sometimes we may
want to give up the struggle. Jesus knows us and offers
us rest. If we just listen to his call to share his yoke and
find peace, we will find life much easier to bear. As we
mature in our walk with Jesus, we will begin to find our
way to living a life of abundance.

"I came so that they might have life and have it
more abundantly."

John 10:10b (NAB)

I believe my dad was a very wise and faith-filled man,
despite the fact he was not very well educated or overly
religious. His actions spoke for themselves. I tried to
learn this from him. Due to my dad's lack of formal

education, however, he would often use a wrong word to express his meaning. Once, many years ago, he and I were discussing how older people begin to lose their thoughts and begin to experience dementia. My dad began telling me about an old customer of his. My dad said: "He has that new disease which sounds like Old Timer's Disease." Of course, he was talking about the devastating Alzheimer's disease.

I once had a friend whose hobby was photography. He told me, "You know that in the end as you grow older, you are left with two things, your memories and your pictures." I once shared this wisdom with my wife, LuAnn, who responded, "Except if you have Alzheimer's disease…With that you lose your memory, and you don't recognize anyone in the pictures." She was right. A sad, but true observation.

> *"I used to make the rules. Now I have to follow other people's rules."*
>
> *(Martin Crane, from the television program Frasier)* [3]

> *"Amen, amen, I say to you, when you were younger, you used to dress yourself and go where you wanted; but when you grow old, you will stretch out your hands, and someone else will dress you and lead you where you do not want to go."*
>
> *John 21:18 (NAB)*

Wisdom comes with age and experience. If you are blessed, you will have a mentor who will enhance your experience and give you wisdom beyond your years. Never forget that you can mentor others and pass along your wisdom to them as well. I feel blessed to have been raised by my parents. Not everyone would have that same opportunity, but all of us can find a mentor in Jesus Christ and the scriptures. Take on his yoke and learn from Jesus, for he is gentle. You will find rest in him. His yoke is easy and his burden is light...

18
"He Is Right...Dead Right"

My dad used this phrase to describe people who were so stubborn about being right that they did do so at their own peril. As an example, in Arizona, as in most states, people have the right-of-way inside a crosswalk. My dad noticed that many people in Arizona would step off of the curb into the crosswalk without watching where they were going or checking to see if traffic was coming in their direction. My dad would say, "Well, it is their right-of-way. If they get run over by a car, they can say they were right...they were dead right."

I have learned from my dad not to be too stubborn about things. Also, not be too stubborn about matters relating to religious and church practices. Now don't get me wrong, piety is a very good virtue, but not if it's compulsive and based in intolerance. Sometimes, it is difficult for people of who were not raised in the Roman Catholic Church or did not go to Catholic schools to understand this point. In the Church, we were taught to memorize our prayers and attend mass on Sunday and other Holy Days of Obligation. We were told where to go and when to be there. We were told not to laugh or talk in church. As I matured in years and in faith, and took classes for the deaconate and spiritual direction, I became less compulsive about my practices of faith and more open to the movement of the Holy Spirit and a genuine relationship with God. For example, I used believe I had to repeat the Rosary every day. Now, of course, I realize that there is nothing wrong with this—except if this practice of faith becomes compulsory for you. You know it is compulsory for you if you begin to think you are committing a sin not to do it—or at the very least, possibly insulting Mary, or worse, insulting God by not doing it. The Church that I grew up in was very good at heaping on this kind of guilt and encouraging these kinds of compulsory faith practices. But by doing so, it led people to believe they could control their relationship with God by their actions. Try to avoid compulsiveness.

We deacons attend a spiritual retreat once a year. On one of those retreats, the retreat master was a well-known author and spiritual director named Fr. Max Oliva (SJ). I remember one very important lesson that he taught on that retreat. He said, "When you're compelled to pray a certain way, at a particular time of day, you experience too much stress over prayer time and miss what the Lord is offering you."

Prayer is a time for communion with God, and time to reflect on what you feel as you pray. Never feel compelled to pray, or you may miss the prompting of the Holy Spirit or the scriptures speaking to you as you read them. I learned that you should always pray with an open heart and open mind to receive what gifts God offers you. When you read scripture, do so without rushing. Pause to reflect when you are moved to do so. Have you ever noticed that sometimes when we read or listen to scripture, there are times when you hear a phrase or a verse you have not heard before, or in the way you are hearing it now, even though you have read that passage many times before? When this happens you should stop reading, go over that passage again, maybe several times, because the Lord is speaking to you in that particular verse. Stop and listen, and reflect on the message. Contained in that passage is a very important lesson that the Lord wants you to hear. You may have passed over that passage before, but this is the time that this passage applies to your life now. So stop, reflect, listen, and let yourself be enriched by this experience. Unfortunately, many people will not do this because they are compelled to complete their reading of the scripture passage, and they will not be distracted. Try being a little looser and more relaxed about your spiritual life, you may find much more of what God wants to offer you. Allow the message of the Lord to engage your heart, not just your mind.

I know that many people are not happy with their prayer life. This could be because they are still praying using the "rote" formula of prayer that they memorized long ago, rather than praying and talking to God from their hearts or their own experience. Let the Spirit move you in your prayer, because we don't even know how to pray or connect to God on our own.

As Paul wrote, "In the same way, the Spirit too comes to the aid of our weakness; for we do not know how to pray as we ought, but the Spirit itself intercedes with inexpressible groanings. And the one who searches hearts knows what is the intention of the Spirit, because

it intercedes for the holy ones according to God's will."
Romans 8: 26-27 (NAB)

I once told my spiritual director that I was not very happy with my prayer life. And she said, "No one is, because prayer is an attempt at communion with God, and we will never be satisfied with our prayer until we can have full communion with God in Heaven."[1]

Saint Augustine prayed, "Our hearts are restless Lord, until they rest in you." [2]

Compulsion has no place in your prayer life. Look at all you could miss. It could even be an occasion for sin. If you let yourself become so compulsive about your practice of prayer and your pious actions, it may cut you off from God. For example, if it causes you to lose your temper with loved ones because they may be interrupting, interfering, or causing you to delay your practice, you have missed the mark. Think about it; that is not the attitude to have when we address the Lord.

O God, please give me patience...and please hurry.

You can be right, but don't be dead right with your prayer and faith practices. Your prayer may reach a dead end.

It's not just in our prayer, but also in life in general, we must not go about our lives compulsively. We must not live so much in our stubbornness and impatience that we miss out on experiencing life and God along the way. I could say to you, "Stop and smell the roses." But you have heard that phrase before and would not listen. Maybe this line from the character Shug in Alice Walker's *The Color Purple*, will get your attention: "I think it [expletive] God off when you walk by the color purple in a field and don't notice it."[3]

My dear Christian friend, God offers us so much. *It's all good.* It is all blessing, and the only way you will ever truly give God thanks is first to notice those gifts.

So, yes. Smell the roses, admire the violets, and thank God for each glorious day.

19
"First Things First"

One lesson my parents taught me was "First things first." When I first heard them say this to me, I was confused about what it meant. As I grew older I disliked that phrase, because it meant that I had to do something that I'd rather not do, or have to put something off until later. Those words, "first things first," helped me not to procrastinate. As Larry the Cable Guy might say, "Git-R-Done."[1]

I have never been a procrastinator. I may have acted too soon at times. I may have leaped before I looked, but I have never procrastinated. Back in the late 1940s, when my parents purchased a corner grocery store, we kids would help around the store. The busiest day for us was when the United Grocery Company would deliver our weekly order of canned goods. Our job was to open the cases of canned goods and stock the shelves. One time, the delivery came a day early, and we did not have a lot of storage space in the stock room. That day we had to open the boxes and stock the shelves the same day of delivery. I remember that delivery day, my brother and I had permission to go to the movies, and we each had twenty-five cents to buy our tickets and candy. Just before leaving for the show (we called the movies "the show" in those days), the United Grocery truck drove up and started to unload. As we began to complain that it was time to leave for the show, our dad said, "First things first...finish the work first." We tried to appeal to him again later in the afternoon. "Come on, Dad, we want to get to the show before the prices change." And our dad would say, "No, get the shelves stocked first. First things first." So we reluctantly went back to work, but that time we worked much faster to get the job done.

You see, we wanted to get to the show before the prices changed, as the daytime shows were at matinee prices, and the prices increased for the evening shows. My kids get a kick out of this, but back in 1949, the theatre in our neighborhood charged only thirteen cents to get into the show before 5:00 p.m. Ticket prices rose to nineteen cents for the evening shows. That does not sound like much money to begin with, and the difference seems insignificant. But to a kid in the late 1940s with only twenty-five cents to spend, it was a big difference. With a quarter, if you could get into the show for thirteen cents, you had twelve cents change to spend on popcorn and candy. Now, my grandchildren wonder why I complain about having to spend $4.00 for a small size popcorn today.

Many years later I was fortunate enough to attend a seminar where the great football coach, motivational speaker, and mentor to thousands of young people Lou Holtz[2] was the keynote speaker. I remember Holtz saying that he thought the key to his success with football teams was that he used the "W.I.N." system of coaching and mentoring people. "W.I.N." was an acronym for "What's

Important Now?" Coach Holtz told us, "On the first day of training camp, I told the team, if you are not sure of what to do next, just ask yourself, what's important now? For instance, when you wake up in the morning, ask yourself, what's important now? Get up and get dressed. Next, W.I.N.? Eat breakfast. Next, what's important now? Get out to the training field, and so on."

Throughout the day you will have decisions to make and many choices to make. Just ask yourself, "What's important now?" Of course, the answer is much the same as what my parents would say: "First things first."

Whether your mentors are leaders like Coach Holtz, or your parents, grandparents, or other life teachers, these people are a blessing for you. Appreciate the mentors in your life, give thanks for joyful abundant living, and remember an attitude of gratitude. Attitude and gratitude are everything. As you pray, pay attention to the things that come up out of your soul. Whether you realize it or not, they expose you to who you are at your inner core and in relation to God.

As a Christian, the good within your heart will also emerge to reveal the goodness and the depth of your love. Your attitude is everything. If you are in gratitude for everything, you will always nurture the love within you and be careful to avoid hate.

"You shall love the Lord, your God, with all your heart, with all your being, with all your strength, and with all your mind, and your neighbor as yourself."

Luke 10:27 (NAB)

Now isn't that a good description of *first things first?*

20
"I Said to Myself, Said I"

My dad would often say, "I said to myself, said I," when he wanted to express his inner thoughts or conversation within himself. He would say this to the delight of us kids. He always made us laugh when he said that. Sometimes Dad would laugh for what seemed like no reason at all, and we would ask him why he was laughing. He would say, "I just told myself a joke." I guess if you can tell yourself jokes, and keep happy thoughts in your mind, you will be living a joyful life. I know that to be true, especially as I observe the people and events in our world today. I am sure you are not surprised...I find a lot humorous things to make me smile and laugh.

We should, however, monitor our self-talk, because our self-talk contributes to our inner attitudes. Also, monitor your inner thoughts about others. Be careful in your heart not to foster hate and contempt for yourself and others. Henri Nouwen once wrote, "The bullet is only the last instrument of hate that began in the heart, long before the bullet left the gun."[1]

I've mentioned Dr. Wayne Dyer earlier in this book, because he has written and taught so many wonderful things over the last forty years. He may be one person that I quoted, or phrase or lesson I mentioned, that I forgot where it originated. It may have been years ago that I made that lesson a part of my life and just forgot where I heard it. One lesson of Dr. Dyer's lessons I shall never forget was that "'you can defuse any argument and keep the peace with these four words: *You're right about that.*"

Sometimes it is more important to keep the peace and avoid an argument with your spouse, your boss, your coworkers, just by saying, "You're right about that." On the other hand, you may want to create stress and argue about your being right. But ask yourself; is this particular issue worth it? You might be right, but as my dad would say, "You could be right...dead right."

Learn a lesson from Jesus Christ and live with humility.

"Why do you notice the splinter in your brother's eye, but do not perceive the wooden beam in your own? How can you say to your brother, 'Brother, let me remove that splinter in your eye,' when you do not even notice the wooden beam in your own eye? You hypocrite. Remove the wooden beam from your eye first; then you will see clearly to remove the splinter in your brother's eye."

Luke 6: 41-42 (NAB)

Oh we love to judge others, don't we? I guess it's because it gives us a sense of superiority. If we, and a few others, can get together and judge another person or group, well, that puts us in a new "elite" class. I don't know about you, but I have a difficult time as it is trying to keep myself in line and living up to my own expectations.

I fall short on so many comparisons with others. I have no room to judge others. I just wish I could be as great a man as my dog thinks I am!

> *"Be merciful, just as (also) your Father is merciful. Stop judging and you will not be judged. Stop condemning and you will not be condemned. Forgive and you will be forgiven. Give and gifts will be given to you; a good measure, packed together, shaken down, and overflowing, will be poured into your lap. For the measure with which you measure will in return be measured out to you."*

> *Luke 6:36-38 (NAB)*

"Wow," I said to myself, said I, "That is a great lesson."

21
"Teach The Right Way The First Time"

As I grew to adolescence and took on more responsibilities around my parents' grocery store, one of my jobs was to break-in new hires. My dad would tell me; "Teach them the right way the first time, then they will learn the shortcuts on their own." What he was teaching me was when you give directions to someone for something, you should always teach the correct and complete way of doing it the first time. That way they know the right way to do it. They know and you know, and there are no questions about it. If you teach the shortcuts or the easy way without the details, that person will never know the right way, or why we do certain things in certain ways. They will find shortcuts and easier ways of doing the same job, and soon the quality of the job begins to suffer.

Now, I am all for doing a job the most efficient and time-saving way, but be careful when teaching the shortcuts, or in the end we may forget how to project what was supposed to be done in the first place. Once in a while, one of the new hires, after being on the job for a short while, would then begin to help a brand-new new hire and show them the ropes, too, so to speak. When this happened, my dad would say, "Look, the blind leading the blind." Often the recent hire would show the new hire the shortcuts he had learned, and the new hire would never learn the correct way of doing things, so quality began to suffer.

Jesus once said, "Can a blind person guide a blind person? Will not both fall into a pit? No disciple is superior to the teacher; but when fully trained, every disciple will be like his teacher." Luke 6:39-40 (NAB)

I have already stated that everybody needs direction; even Christians need spiritual direction. Jesus came to awaken His people, and to show the way. But which is the right way? Some say the scriptures show the way, others say the pope will show the way, still others say they follow a particular preacher who seems to know the way. There is a little story that was used to make a point about religious intolerance in part of a poem written by John Godfrey Saxe, in eighteenth-century England. It reads:

It was six men of Indostan, to learning much inclined, who went to see the Elephant (though all of them were blind), and that each by observation might satisfy his mind.

The First approached the Elephant, and happening to fall against his broad and sturdy side, at once began to bawl: "God bless me. But the Elephant is very like a wall."

The Second, feeling of the tusk, cried: "Ho. What have we here? So very round and smooth and sharp? To me 'tis mighty clear, this wonder of an Elephant is very like a spear."

The Third approached the animal and happening to take the squirming trunk within his hands, thus boldly up and spoke: "I see, the Elephant is very like a snake."

The Fourth reached out an eager hand, and felt about the knee: "What most this wondrous beast is like is mighty plain, 'tis clear enough the Elephant is very like a tree."

The Fifth, who chanced to touch the ear, said: "Even the blindest man can tell what this resembles most; deny the fact, who can, this marvel of an Elephant is very like a fan."

The Sixth no sooner had begun about the beast to grope, then, seizing on the swinging tail that fell within his scope: "I see, the Elephant is very like a rope."

And so these men of Indostan disputed loud and long, each in his own opinion exceeding stiff and strong, though each was partly in the right, and all were in the wrong.

MORAL:

So often in theological wars the disputants, I wean, rail on in utter ignorance of what each other mean; and prate about an Elephant not one of them has seen."[1]

The lesson here is how do you experience God? None of us can experience the whole of God. I believe God is so multifaceted that each person, each Christian church, can experience only a part of God.

Jesus Christ, who became the personification of God, said, "I am the way and the truth and the life. No one comes to the Father except through me. If you know me, then you will also know my Father. From now on you do know him and have seen him." John 14:6-7 (NAB)

But many people do not know or believe in the Christ, so are they lost? Many people experience our Heavenly Father in various ways. Is there another way? God only knows those who will find the way to salvation. But one thing we do know is that Jesus Christ is the truth, the way, and the life for those who believe. We need spiritual direction, or it could be easy to get lost. Most people sleepwalk through life, but Jesus came to wake us up. We who follow Christ have been given the same mandate. We, through the power of the Holy Spirit, are to wake others and show them the way. We must show them the right way the first time. God knows we humans are always looking for shortcuts.

Someone asked Jesus, "Lord, will only a few people be saved?" He answered them, "Strive to enter through the narrow gate, for many, I tell you, will attempt to enter but will not be strong enough." Luke 13:23-24 (NAB)

There are numerous opinions among Christians about the number to be saved. Some believe few will be saved.

Others believe all will be saved, many fall somewhere in the middle or think the question is poorly posed. It is not desirable to explain away these points of genuine difference here, for there can be no agreement. For the perfect guide turn to Jesus Christ the Good Shepherd. Please read and reflect on Psalm 23 below.

> *"The LORD is my shepherd; there is nothing I lack. In green pastures you let me graze; to safe waters you lead me; you restore my strength. You guide me along the right path for the sake of your name. Even when I walk through a dark valley, I fear no harm for you are at my side; your rod and staff give me courage. You set a table before me as my enemies watch; you anoint my head with oil; my cup overflows. Only goodness and love will pursue me all the days of my life; I will dwell in the house of the LORD for years to come."*
>
> *Psalm 23 (NAB)*

> *"For the Son of Man has come to seek and to save what was lost."*
>
> *Luke 19: 10 (NAB)*

22
"Taking Care of Business"

"Take care of business, and the business will take care of you."

My dad was *not* the first to coin that phrase, but he sure liked to use it, and he wanted me to believe it, too. During World War II, people at the home front were encouraged to grow their own backyard gardens to assist the war effort. They called these gardens "victory gardens." My dad used to say, "I am growing a victory garden, but the weeds are winning."

Gardens are like life. You have to stick with it, and work it, and nurture it like anything else in this world. "Take care of the garden and the garden will take care of you." This saying is true on so many levels in our lives and culture. I would like to apply it to a life in faith. I do believe that like everything else in life, a Christian's faith is a gift. And as with all gifts, we can squander it or nurture it. Unfortunately, since many of us first discover our faith when we are young children, many people associate a strong faith with childhood fantasy and do not take it seriously. Unfortunately, folks who think this way have either lost their faith or never had it to begin with. That is sad to me. When I think of them, I have to ask, "In what do they believe?" If you don't believe in something, you will fall for anything.

If you take care of your faith, your faith will take care of you. When you nurture your gift of faith, it will bless you in so many ways. It will affect your attitude about everything.

I would like to share a story of attitude, gratitude, faith, courage in relation to the idea of "taking care of business."

As my dad grew older, he developed colon cancer and had to have a section of his colon removed. All of his family gathered in the hospital waiting room to wait and pray as he had surgery. Finally, we were told that the operation was a success. All went well, except the doctor could not reconnect his colon, as it was too close to the rectum, which meant my dad would have a colostomy and wear a colostomy bag for the rest of his life. We were concerned for my dad because mom had passed away before him, and he would be living alone and dealing with this condition himself.

We could not see him immediately because he was in recovery. But when they did move him to a room, I was the first to go in and see him. Since he was still under some anesthesia, I just sat quietly with him and prayed. A short time later, I saw his eyes open, and as he recognized me, he said "Bill, did they tell you how the operation came out?" I said yes, and then he said sleepily, "I guess I'll have to do a little business on the side." Wow! *That* was my dad, always a positive attitude, always courageous, and always taking care of business.

Attitude is everything—gratitude for everything.

Keep this in mind, and you will be blessed in all areas of your life. My mom was a great cook even though she did not have much at home when growing up, as there was not a lot of food or many opportunities to cook in her house. But after she married my dad, her Italian mother-in-law, my Nanna Catherine, taught her how to prepare my dad's favorite dishes. Then, after Nanna died, my parents bought the grocery store, and never again was she short of any ingredients for her recipes.

One of my dad's favorite dishes was gnocchi, those little potato dumplings covered with my mom's best sauce. As a child I remember thinking what funny-sounding name gnocchi was. None of my non-Italian friends had ever heard that word or knew what I was talking about, so they could never understand how mmm-mmm good they were. It's interesting to me how gnocchi is now on gourmet menus in the better Italian restaurants today.

Because my parents spent so much time at their grocery store, my mom did not have a lot of time to prepare homemade pasta dishes like my dad's favorite gnocchi. So, often she would prepare her dishes the night before serving them. I remember this one time when she prepared the uncooked gnocchi dumplings and put them in the refrigerator so that she could prepare and serve them for dinner the next day. At the time, my sister Vivian and I attended grade school while my parents worked at the store. Vivian and I would get home from school several hours before our parents got home from the store. Like most children, we came home famished and went through the kitchen and refrigerator looking for something to eat. Now, you should know that I was known to eat the pasta dough and cookie dough while my mom was preparing it, and often she would scold me or smack my fingers with the spatula or some other kitchen utensil. Come to think of it, my wife does the same thing today. Anyway, this one time I spied the pan of gnocchi in the refrigerator. I knew that they were made for that night's supper, and I did not touch the gnocchi, even though I wanted to. I know my mom would not appreciate that, so I did not even try.

When my parents got home that night and supper was being prepared. My mom noticed that the top layer of the dumplings was short one row. She thought that I had eaten the row of gnocchi dough. This upset her, and when she confronted me about it, I told her that I had not touched the gnocchi and had noticed that same row missing when I looked in the refrigerator earlier as well. Now my mom became angry with me because she thought I was lying, and as she questioned me further, I kept denying that I ate the gnocchi dough. Now, we rarely lied to our parents, and I was telling the truth for sure this time. My mom sent me to bed right then and there. That was the first time I was ever sent to bed without my supper. I think my mom and I were both crying as I went to my bedroom. As I lay in bed crying, hungry, and missing out on my beloved gnocchi, I could not believe this was happening to me. If you knew me, you would know that I have not missed too many meals. Well, the time passed by, supper was over and it was now early evening, when my mom came into my room and asked if

I was asleep. I said no, she said to me, "Why don't you get up and eat, and then you can watch TV until bedtime. I am sorry that I accused you and thought that you were lying to me." On top of that we hugged and made up and I got to eat my leftover gnocchi. Later, after I ate, I was sitting in the family room watching TV with my dad. My dad told me that my mom came to him and said, "Vic, I think I may have been wrong, I thought there were two full layers of gnocchi in that pan, but maybe I made a mistake." My dad said: "Well, get him up and give him his dinner, we should have known better, he never lies to us."

Like in business, if you take care of your reputation, it will take care of you.

23

"Two Wrongs Don't Make A Right"

My dad would make this point any time he wanted to correct our behavior when we would desire to exact revenge on a person who may have hurt us initially. He would say, "Two wrongs don't make a right."

This was his attempt to keep his kids always doing the right thing. He would tell us stories of others' mistakes and try to help us avoid the same mistakes. I loved his stories and how he used them to teach us a lesson. As I got older and became a father myself, I would use those stories to help my children to better learn a lesson. Also, I realized that Jesus used stories to teach his followers. One of my favorite stories is found in Luke's Gospel titled "The Lost Son (Prodigal) and The Dutiful Son." Many know this as the story of the Prodigal Son. The word "prodigal" can mean "wasteful" or "extravagant." Of the three main characters in the story—the lost son, the dutiful son, and the father—to me, it is the father who is the most extravagant. Maybe the story should be called "The Parable of the Prodigal Father." Because the father in the story represents God our Heavenly Father, and the parable describes his extravagant love for us. To better understand why I say this, let's take a good look at Luke's passage:

A man had two sons, and the younger son
said to his father, "Father, give me the share
of your estate that should come to me." So the
father divided the property between them.
After a few days, the younger son collected all
his belongings and set off to a distant country
where he squandered his inheritance on a life of
dissipation. When he had freely spent everything,
a severe famine struck that country, and he
found himself in dire need. So he hired himself
out to one of the local citizens who sent him to
his farm to tend the swine. And he longed to eat
his fill of the pods on which the swine fed, but
nobody gave him any. Coming to his senses, he
thought, 'How many of my father's hired workers
have more than enough food to eat, but here am
I, dying from hunger. I shall get up and go to my
father and I shall say to him, "Father, I have
sinned against heaven and against you. I no
longer deserve to be called your son; treat me as
you would treat one of your hired workers."' So
he got up and went back to his father. While he
was still a long way off, his father caught sight
of him, and was filled with compassion. He ran
to his son, embraced him, and kissed him. His
son said to him, 'Father, I have sinned against
heaven and against you; I no longer deserve to
be called your son.' But his father ordered his
servants, 'Quickly bring the finest robe and put
it on him; put a ring on his finger and sandals

*on his feet. Take the fattened calf and slaughter
it. Then let us celebrate with a feast, because
this son of mine was dead, and has come to life
again; he was lost, and has been found.' Then
the celebration began. Now the older son had
been out in the field and, on his way back, as he
neared the house, he heard the sound of music
and dancing. He called one of the servants and
asked what this might mean. The servant said to
him, 'Your brother has returned and your father
has slaughtered the fattened calf because he has
him back safe and sound.' He became angry, and
when he refused to enter the house, his father
came out and pleaded with him. He said to his
father in reply, "Look, all these years I served
you and not once did I disobey your orders; yet
you never gave me even a young goat to feast on
with my friends. But when your son returns who
swallowed up your property with prostitutes,
for him you slaughter the fattened calf." He said
to him, "My son, you are here with me always;
everything I have is yours. But now we must
celebrate and rejoice, because your brother was
dead and has come to life again; he was lost and
has been found."*

Luke 15:11-32 (NAB)

This parable is a good example of my dad's saying,
"Two wrongs don't make a right." First, the younger
son goes to his father and says, "Father, give me my

share of the estate that is coming to me." What he is really saying is "Dad, I really can't wait for you to die, so give me my inheritance now." I know that my son Victor would never say such a thing. If he did, I would smack him upside the head. But then again, I am not the extravagant father. As we know from the story, his father divides his property and gives the younger son his share. As we know, the younger son squanders and wastes his fortune on reckless living. After going broke and starving, the younger son goes to work for a local farmer to feed pigs. This was like adding insult to injury for a Jew, and yet, he longed to eat the pig's food. Finally, coming to his senses, he decides to return to his father. Then, the father is longing for his son and is staring into the distance when he sees him coming home. The father runs out to meet him (a mature man and a wealthy man in that culture never would run), and he embraces his son. Of course, the father in the story represents God, our Heavenly Father. Sometimes this same thing happens to us while praying. We realize that the God whom we pursue is actually pursuing us.

As the father and son embrace, the young man tries to apologize and ask for his forgiveness. But the father ignores him. He puts a ring on his finger, sandals on his feet, and orders his best robe for the son to wear. And then he orders the fatted calf to be killed and roasted and a celebration to begin.

Now the dutiful son comes in from the fields and hears the sounds of celebration coming from the house. He inquires and finds out from a servant that the father is celebrating because he has his son back home safe. The dutiful son refuses to join in the celebration. His father comes out of the house to plead with him to come into the house to celebrate his brother's return, but the dutiful son refuses, telling his father, that this son of his has wasted his money on wild living and prostitutes. But the loving extravagant father reassures the dutiful son. He tells him that everything that he has is his, but that they must rejoice and celebrate, because we have your brother safely home. "Your brother was dead and has come to life again; he was lost and has been found." Luke 15:32 (NAB)

In the end, both of these sons are spoiled and ungrateful to their loving, generous, and extravagant father. In spite of their hurtful actions and words, the father still loved and forgave the repentant son. This story is an example of our Heavenly Father's love and mercy, and the rejoicing over the repentant sinner.

"For the Son of Man has come to seek and to save what was lost."

Luke 19:10 (NAB)

The story of the two sons is a good example of, how two wrongs don't make a right. It is fortunate that the two sons had a loving father who could make all things right—as it can be for you, too.

24
"Faith, Hope, and Love"

When my daughter Nancy was a senior in high school, she had to have a tutor come to the house. We had earlier moved our family out of her high school district, so in order for this arrangement to work, Nancy had to meet the tutor at my parents' house, as my parents lived across the street from her high school. This gave Nancy a wonderful opportunity visit her "Gram" and "Pap" every school-day afternoon.

As a related story, you should know we did not call my parents Nanna and Nonno like they did in my dad's family. When my older brother Ed and his wife Bea began a family, their first child, Kathy, could not say "Grand Pap!" So she would call my dad "Pap-Pap!" So that name stuck and all of the grandchildren called my dad "Pap-Pap!" When my own grandchildren came along, they called me "Pap," and my dad "Pap-Pap." Once, my youngest grandson, Anthony, was asking my oldest grandson, Nicholas, about something that I had said, and Nicholas asked, "Who are you talking about, Pap, or Double Pap?" I just wanted to share that because I thought it was a cute story.

So every day after school, Nancy would have the opportunity to visit with my parents while waiting for the tutor. The year was 1982, the last year of my mother's life, and it made Nancy so grateful to be able to spend so much time with them that year.

As I was writing this book, I asked Nancy what she might want to share about her grandparents for the book. She told me that she was struck by their love and devotion for one another and the joy they shared. They lived lives of faith, hope, and love, and they shared that with their family. The Apostle Paul wrote these words in scripture two thousand years ago:

"If I speak in human and angelic tongues but do not have love, I am a resounding gong or a clashing cymbal. And if I have the gift of prophecy and comprehend all mysteries and all knowledge; if I have all faith so as to move mountains but do not have love, I am nothing. If I give away everything I own, and if I hand my body over so that I may boast but do not have love, I gain nothing. Love is patient, love is kind. It is not jealous, (love) is not pompous, it is not inflated, it is not rude, it does not seek its own interests, it is not quick-tempered, it does not brood over injury, it does not rejoice over wrongdoing but rejoices with the truth. It bears all things, believes all things, hopes all things, endures all things. Love never fails. If there are prophecies, they will be brought to nothing; if tongues, they will cease; if knowledge, it will be brought to nothing. For we know partially and we prophesy partially, but when the perfect comes, the partial will pass away. When I was a child, I used to talk as a

*child, think as a child, reason as a child; when
I became a man, I put aside childish things. At
present we see indistinctly, as in a mirror, but
then face to face. At present I know partially; then
I shall know fully, as I am fully known. So faith,
hope, love remain, these three; but the greatest of
these is love."*

1 Corinthians 13:1-13 (NAB)

This beautiful scripture is often read at weddings because it describes perfect love. In it, the Apostle Paul is describing the love that the Father has for us, and the love that Christians should have for one another. These are more than beautiful words, they are very powerful words, and were meant to go far beyond the wedding day. In fact, a wedding ceremony was not even in Paul's thoughts when he wrote these words. Yet, a loving relationship between a man and a woman is the epitome of love, if done well.

I enjoy a story that I once heard about a couple celebrating their fortieth wedding anniversary.

*This couple arrived home late and exhausted
after a night out celebrating with their family and
friends. The husband offered to make a snack for
both of them before they went up to bed. The wife
slumped on the stool by the kitchen bar while he
went to the refrigerator and brought out the sliced
ham, cheese, and condiments to make them each
a sandwich. When he went to the bread box to
retrieve the sliced bread, he found only the last*

four slices. He proceeded to make the sandwiches and put them on plates and cut them just the way his wife liked it. As he slid the plate with her sandwich on it over to her, she said, "The heel of the bread? You always give me the heel of the bread. After all of these years, I have not said anything to you about it, but I hate the heel of the bread. Honey, why do you always give me the heel of the bread?" He answered rather sheepishly, "I...I always give you the heel of the bread because that is my favorite part."

When I officiate at a wedding, the couple may not always choose to have the Apostle Paul's reading from 1 Corinthians 13 read at the wedding, but I always tell the story of the love and devotion of that couple and the ham sandwiches. And when I counsel young couples who are preparing for marriage, I try to emphasize the importance of good communication skills. If couples would communicate their love and desires, their likes and dislikes, their hopes and dreams, their chances of a good marriage is greatly enhanced. If the couple in my little story had better communication skills, the angst over the heel of the bread could have been avoided altogether. Couples should begin their marriage with good communication because they love one another, and out of that love and respect, should be able to communicate all of their concerns. When you love someone, your desire is their happiness, but also you should share your own desires. You should be able to honestly communicate about children, sex, finances, or whatever, because the two of you are "one" when you are married.

"That is why a man leaves his father and mother and clings to his wife, and the two of them become one body."

Genesis 2:24 (NAB)

My mom died at age sixty-five in 1982, just as she and my dad were about to celebrate their forty-fifth wedding anniversary. As I write this book, I am sixty-five years old, and LuAnn and I are about to celebrate forty-five years of marriage ourselves. My wife and I are in good health, and I expect that we will be celebrating our fiftieth anniversary in five more years. LuAnn and I know that every day is precious, and like my parents, we try to be devoted to one another and live our lives filled with faith, hope, and love.

As Paul writes, "So faith, hope, love remain, these three; but the greatest of these is love." 1 Corinthians 13:13 (NAB)

25

"Que Sera Sera"

(Whatever will be, will be...)[1]

My parents would say these words long before Doris Day sang them in her big hit song in the 1950s. They would say, "Why worry? You don't have control over your fate." But you do have control of your faith. My parents had faith. They had faith in God, faith in their country, and faith in each other, and they tried to pass this steady faith of theirs on to their children. I don't really know if their faith was ever shaken. If it was, they did not show it. If one of us kids came to them with a concern, they would listen, and with certainty would then say, "Don't worry, it will be all right." Or they would say, *"Que sera sera"* (whatever will be, will be.) Just trust that everything will be okay. It is all in the hands of God. I have learned life is just a matter of knowing who you are—then in difficult times, remembering who you are. Who are you? As a Christian, you carry the Spirit of God within you.

The LORD God formed man out of the clay of the ground and blew into his nostrils the breath of life, and so man became a living being.

Genesis 2:7 (NAB)

First man was created in God's image, and then God breathed the breath of life into him. Now, you might say, what happened? Well, as the story goes, man fell from grace through deception. God equipped us with what we needed to survive. He also gave us the means of salvation, but many choose the darkness over the light. Those of you who have children may be able to better understand our human nature. How many parents have given their children all that they need to not only survive, but to grow and prosper, and to be educated and to contribute to the world? How many parents know what it is like to be told by their children in return, "Thanks, but, no thanks." to their generosity? But God did not give up on His children. He is always with us and will always be with us as long as we breathe, because we breathe the "breath of life." This truth is brought forth in the Gospel of John:

> *All things came to be through him, and without him nothing came to be. What came to be through him was life, and this life was the light of the human race. The light shines in the darkness, and the darkness has not overcome it.*

John 1:4-5 (NAB)

and

> *The true light, which enlightens everyone, was coming into the world.*

John 1:9 (NAB)

and

But to those who did accept him he gave power to become children of God, to those who believe in his name.

John 2:12 (NAB)

This, as a Christian, if you can believe it and accept it, this is who you are:

You are an embodied soul....

You carry the Spirit of God within you...

You also carry his light within you, so, let it shine.

Remember this little song from Sunday school? "This little light of mine, I'm gonna let it shine. Let it shine, let it shine, let it shine."

If you have not thought about these things in a while, now is the time. Don't hide your light any longer. Let it shine, let it shine, let it shine. Don't worry about where all of this will lead—*Que sera sera.*

There is a little story that I once heard about how a new mother had gone to the nursery to see her newborn child, and was surprised to see that her four-year-old son was standing next to the crib and was whispering to his baby sister. The mother asked her little boy, "What were you talking to the baby about?" He answered, "Oh, I just asked her to tell me what God is like. I forgot."

If God knew us before we were formed in our mother's womb, did we know him? Did we forget?

"Before I formed you in the womb I knew you..."

Jeremiah 1:5a (NAB)

and...

*"You formed my inmost being; you knit me in my
mother's womb. I praise you, so wonderfully you
made me; wonderful are your works. My very self
you knew."*

Psalm 139:13-14 (NAB)

As we get further along in life, we do get caught up
with the business of living. But it would be good, every
once in a while, to do some remembering with our true
center. Remember who you are.

*Jesus said to them again: "Peace be with you. As
the Father has sent me, so I send you." and when
he had said this, he breathed on them and said
to them, "Receive the holy Spirit."*

John 20:21-22 (NAB)

The Kingdom of God is near; it is so near that, as a
Christian, it is within you. If you don't know that, try to
understand the gift the Father has desired to give you:
pray about it, study it, discuss it with your spiritual
director, and believe.

I don't know all the ways I have come to these
understandings, but I know them to be true. I am hoping
you will, too. I have been blessed by "my father's wisdom
and my mother's love" —and now you have, too.

Go now in peace and love. *Que Sera Sera...*

Vic and Mary Vivio at their granddaughters'
Kathy and Rhonda's combined wedding reception.
March 8, 1980

End Notes

Scripture texts in this work are taken from the *New American Bible with Revised New Testament* © 1986, 1970 Confraternity of Christian Doctrine, Washington, D.C.

United States Conference of Catholic Bishops
3211 4th Street, N.E., Washington, DC 20017-1194
(202) 541-3000
November 11, 2002
Copyright © by United States Conference of Catholic Bishops.

V

1. Merton, Thomas. *New Seeds of Contemplation.* New York: New Directions Publishing, 1972.

Introduction

1. Emerson, Ralph Waldo (1803–1882). Born in Boston, MA. American poet, philosopher, essayist, and author.
2. Robert, Cavett (1908-1997). Born in Mississippi. Founded the National Speakers Association, 1972.

Chapter 1

1. Dyer, Wayne W. Public Broadcasting Services (PBS) Program, date unknown.
2. Lyte, Eliphalet O. "Row, Row, Row Your Boat." New York: The Franklin Square Song Collection, 1881.
3. O'Malley, William, S.J. *Pursuit of Happiness: Evolving a Soul.* Texas: Thomas More Pr, 1995.

Chapter 2
1. Attributed to MacDonald, George (1824–1905), Scottish author, poet, and Christian minister.

Chapter 3
1. Attributed to McCarthy, J.J. (O Carm). Pastor, St. Bernadette Church, Houston, Texas.
2. Attributed to Terry, Randall A. (born 1959). Pro-life activist, author, and musician.

Chapter 4
1. Unknown.

Chapter 5
1. Samuel Ichiye Hayakawa (1906–1992). Canadian-born American academic author and political figure.
2. Merton, Thomas (1915–1968). Born in France, Trappist monk, author, and poet.

Chapter 6
1. *The Godfather* (1972). Don Vito Corleone (portrayed by Marlon Brando).
2. *The Godfather Part II* (1974). Michael Corleone (portrayed by Al Pacino).
3. Nouwen, Henri J. M. (1932–1996). Priest, professor, and author.

Chapter 7
1. Fr. Dominic Valentino (1919–2001). Born in Chicago, IL. Catholic priest and pastor.
2. Unknown.

Chapter 8

1. Unknown.
2. Willie Nelson. "Forgiving Is Easy," from "Revolutions of time—Journey 1975–1993'. Released in1995.

Chapter 10

1. St. Augustine, Bishop of Hippo (354–430). Born in Algiers, Africa. Ordained a priest 390, and bishop 396.

Chapter 12

1. Unknown.
2. Rohr, Richard (OFM), born in Kansas, MO in 1943.
3. Nouwen, Henri J. M. Born and educated in Holland. Ordained a priest in 1957, taught at Notre Dame and Yale universities.
4. Bumper sticker from George's South Side (restaurant and bar). Baton Rouge, LA.
5. Hinton, Hilary ("Zig" Ziglar). Born November 6, 1926. American author, salesperson, and motivational speaker.

Chapter 13

1. *Training Day* (2001). Alonzo Harris (portrayed by Denzel Washington).
2. Nouwen, Henri J. M. *With Burning Hearts: A Meditation on the Eucharistic Life.* New York: Orbis Books. 2003 Audio book

Chapter 15

1. St. Irenaues lived circa 130–178. Bishop and martyr.
2. Dale Carnegie Course: Effective Communications & Human Relations.

3. Carnegie, Dale. *How to Stop Worrying and Start Living*. Dale. Simon and Schuster, 1990.
4. Carnegie, Dale. *How to Stop Worrying and Start Living*. Dale. Simon and Schuster, 1990.

Chapter 17
1. Artist: Tony Bennett as sung on "Tony Bennett's Greatest Hits, Vol. III" Columbia (CL 2313) - peaked Billboard position # 70 in 1963 also charted in 1963 by Burl Ives at # 63 - Words and Music by Gordon Jenkins.
2. Barrow, Joseph Louis (1914–1981). "The Brown Bomber." Heavyweight boxing champion.
3. *Frasier*. Marty Crane (portrayed by John Mahoney).

Chapter 18
1. Spangler, Sharon, friend and spiritual director.
2. St. Augustine, Bishop of Hippo (354–430). Born in Algiers, Africa. Ordained a priest 390, and bishop 396.
3. Walker, Alice. *The Color Purple*. Pocket Books, 1982.

Chapter 19
1. Larry the Cable Guy (portrayed by comedian Daniel Lawrence Whitney).
2. Holtz, Louis Leo, American football coach.

Chapter 20
1. Nouwen, Henri J. M. (1932–1996). Born in Holland. Ordained in 1957. Catholic priest, professor, and author.

Chapter 21

1. Saxe, John Godfrey (1816–1887). "Indian Legend." Published in Linton's Poetry of America, 1878.

Chapter 25

1. "Que Sera Sera (Whatever Will Be, Will Be)." Published in 1956. A popular song by Jay Livingston (music) and Ray Evans (lyrics).

About the Author

Bill Vivio was born in Pittsburgh, Pennsylvania, on April 7, 1942. He was raised in the family grocery business. Bill, his brother Ed, and his sister Vivian did all of the various chores associated with a family business to help their parents, Victor and Mary Vivio, run their store.

Bill married the love of his life, LuAnn Yacono, on July 4, 1963; they raised three children, Nancy, Gina, and Victor. The family moved to Phoenix, Arizona, in 1972, where Bill began a career in insurance and real estate.

Bill and LuAnn were active members at Saint Helen's Catholic Church in Glendale, Arizona. Their pastor, Fr. Edward Wjada, suggested that Bill enroll in classes to become a deacon for the Diocese of Phoenix. As Bill likes to say, "In 1977, the same year that Elvis died and *Star Wars* was born, I was ordained a Permanent Deacon."

Bill later took studies at the Kino Institute in Phoenix, Arizona, and San Diego University, and the Spiritual Ministry Center, also in San Diego, to become a spiritual director. After thirty years of working in various ministries in the Catholic Church, Bill is publishing his first book, *My Father's Wisdom and My Mother's Love: A Spiritual Gift.*

Today Bill is retired from his real estate career and enjoying life with his family, which now includes his four grandchildren, Nicholas, Stephanie, Anthony, and Megan.